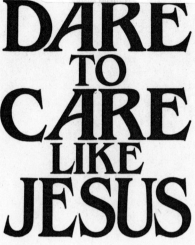

DARE TO CARE LIKE JESUS

Leslie B. Flynn

This book is designed for your personal reading pleasure and profit. It is also designed for group study. A leader's guide with helps and hints for teachers and visual aids (Victor Multiuse Transparency Masters) is available from your local bookstore or from the publisher.

VICTOR

BOOKS a division of SP Publications, Inc.
WHEATON, ILLINOIS 60187

Offices also in
Whitby, Ontario, Canada
Amersham-on-the-Hill, Bucks, England

Second printing, 1983

Unless otherwise noted, Scripture quotations are from the *King James Version*. Other quotations are from the *New International Version* (NIV), © 1978 by the New York International Bible Society; *The Holy Bible: Revised Standard Version* (RSV), © 1952 by the Division of Christian Education of the National Council of the Churches of Christ in the United States; and the *New English Bible* (NEB), © The Delegates of the Oxford University Press, 1961, 1970. Used by permission.

Recommended Dewey Decimal Classification: 248.4
  Suggested Subject Headings: CHRISTIAN LIFE; BEHAVIOR; SPIRITUAL LIFE

Library of Congress Catalog Card Number: 81-51949
ISBN: 0-88207-348-6

© 1982 by SP Publications, Inc. All rights reserved
Printed in the United States of America

VICTOR BOOKS
A division of SP Publications, Inc.
P.O. Box 1825 • Wheaton, Illinois 60187

Contents

Contents

To our senior deacon,
James A. Gray,
a caring gentleman
of Scottish descent.

1
The Tears
of Jesus

Recently I sat on the platform of Philpott Memorial Church in Hamilton, Ontario, Canada, scheduled to deliver the morning sermon. Suddenly, during a hymn, as my eyes swept over this familiar scene, recognizing friends of other years, memories began to flow.

This was the church where I had received all my Christian training for the first 18 years of my life. I had been brought there to Sunday School as a child. I glanced at the pew where I had sat beside my mother every Sunday morning and evening year after year. I gazed at the aisle down which my father had ushered for 40 years. Then I looked at the back seat of the balcony from which I had responded to the Gospel at age 15. I thought of the Wednesday night youth group where I had received my first training in giving Bible talks. I remembered leaving this church to go away to Moody Bible Institute. Though away from this church for 40 years, I had often filled the pulpit on annual visits to my parents till their deaths eight years ago. Looking out over the congregation, I missed my mother and father. Memories so overwhelmed me that I felt tears running down my cheeks.

Then I remembered something else. Men shouldn't cry. American society frowns on male tears, linking them to weakness, dependence, or childishness. I reached for my handkerchief and dabbed at my eyes and cheeks. As I rose to speak, a malfunction in the loud-speaking system quickly jolted me back to masculine composure.

But tough guys *do* cry. One of pro football's greatest linebackers was Sam Huff, iron man and tough guy who played in 157 consecutive NFL games. Before announcing his decision to retire, he spent 15 minutes alone in front of his locker, crying.

Tears often provide an emotional safety valve. Some physical illnesses are intensified by failure to find escape in tears. The lump in the throat, the band tightening around the heart, and the weight on the chest can all stem from rigid emotional control.

Still many people find it almost impossible to cry. A 19-year-old girl in London, England won $33,000 in damages in a lawsuit, but she was unable to weep for joy at the verdict. Because of head injuries she suffered when struck by a truck three years before, she could no longer shed tears. Isn't she symbolic of thousands who, in winning wealth or success, become utterly unfeeling and tearless in the process?

It's so easy for us to harden our hearts against the stern realities of life and the misfortunes of others till we find ourselves cold, calloused, and cryless. Our hearts are far removed from the days of the prophets, when long periods of weeping and mourning over wrongdoing were common. Most Bible characters wept including Abraham, Jacob, Joseph, Moses, Saul, David, Elijah, Peter, Paul, and John.

But most significant of all, the Lord Jesus Christ wept at least on three occasions.

At a Grave

Away in Perea because of the hostile atmosphere around Jerusalem, Jesus received word of Lazarus' illness. "Behold, he whom Thou lovest is sick" (John 11:3). Jesus' two-day delay before starting out for Bethany must have puzzled the disciples. Their bewilderment increased on finding Lazarus dead.

Some think Jesus delayed arrival till the fourth day to avoid those first three frenzied days of the month-long mourning period. But the real reason was to provide opportunity for Jesus to perform His greatest miracle, raising a man who had lain four days in the grave. He had told the disciples when they learned of Lazarus' illness that death would not be the final outcome of this illness; rather that its culmination would be the glory of God (vv. 4, 15).

At Jesus' arrival, Martha and Mary spoke to Him separately. Baffled, but not bitter, both said, "Lord, if Thou hadst been here, my brother had not died" (vv. 21, 32). Jesus asked, "Where have ye laid him?" They answered, "Come and see" (v. 34). Then we read those majestic words, "Jesus wept" (v. 35). Down those holy cheeks trickled tears. Bystanders remarked, "Behold how He loved him!" (v. 36).

Even though He knew He was about to perform a mighty miracle and raise Lazarus from the dead, Jesus' heart was overwhelmed with genuine sorrow. Unlike the crocodile tears of the professional mourners, His were real. When a moment later His voice, with the power of deity, called Lazarus back from the dead, His face was still stained with the tears of His humanity.

We need to weep in the hour of sorrow. Mistakenly, some think it unchristian to shed tears, but spiritual to keep a stiff upper lip when a loved one passes away. Perhaps the error arose from a misplaced comma. Paul, writing to the Thessalonian believers concerning their dead, urged "that ye sorrow not, even as others which have no hope" (1Thes. 4:13). To give proper meaning the comma ought to come one word earlier so that the verse would read, "that you sorrow, not even as others which have no hope." Sorrow is natural, but the believer has supernatural hope.

When Stephen was stoned to death, "devout men . . . made great lamentation over him" (Acts 8:2). Noisy wailings accompanied the death of the first Christian martyr. When Dorcas, a godly woman died, before Peter brought her back from the dead, "all the widows stood by him weeping, and showing the coats and garments" which she had made (9:39). Jesus, too, wept at the loss of a loved one. Weeping in the hour of sorrow *is* Christlike. In order to handle grief, it must be expressed. When Augustine's mother died, he was overwhelmed with sorrow, for their relationship had been close. In his *Confessions* he tells how he squelched his feelings, thinking he would spoil his Christian witness before the pagans by crying. But holding back the flood of tears brought on a depression, as the bitterness of sorrow festered within his heart. Not till he gave unrestrained vent to his grief did he find peace again.

Jesus said, "Blessed are they that mourn: for they shall be comforted" (Matt. 5:4). As He wept along with Martha and Mary, so He weeps with us in our times of grief. The unseen mourner at every funeral, He cares when we say good-bye to the dearest on earth to us.

We need to weep with those that weep. After the death of her husband, a mother was challenged by her daughter, "Mother, you didn't really love Daddy. You never cried."

"Oh, but darling, I did cry. Many a night I cried myself to sleep. I never wanted to break down in front of you."

"Mother, I'm sorry I misjudged you. But I wish you had cried with me, and not alone."

Over a City

The second instance of Jesus weeping could be termed "tears midst triumph." He was about to enter Jerusalem for a so-called victorious reception on what we call Palm Sunday. Reaching a turn in the road in His descent from the Mount of Olives, and catching a view of the whole city before Him, He began to weep (Luke 19:41).

Though the crowd was about to exclaim "Hosanna," Jesus knew that in a few days many of the same mob would shout "Crucify Him!" The verb used here for weeping differs from that used to describe the sorrow at Lazarus' grave where He shed tears silently. Here, over the city He sobbed audibly, "If thou hadst known, even thou, at least in this thy day, the things which belong unto thy peace! But now they are hid from thine eyes" (vv. 41-42).

Jerusalem means "city of peace." But its history had been anything but peaceful. Jerusalem had been captured, destroyed, rebuilt, captured again, despoiled, and was under Roman yoke during Jesus' time. But sadder still, the people had forgotten their God. Ritual abounded, but little righteousness. Jesus had come with a message of life, but scorning Him, the authorities were plotting to kill Him. Now with their opportunity for real peace, the people failed to recognize the Prince of Peace.

Jesus not only lamented their blindness, but also their fate. "For the days shall come upon thee, that thine enemies shall cast a trench about thee, and compass thee round, and keep thee in on every side, and shall lay thee even with the ground, and thy children within thee; and they shall not leave in thee one stone upon another; because thou knewest not the time of thy visitation" (vv. 43-44).

Jesus could see ahead to the siege of Jerusalem by the Roman army under Vespasian and Titus in A.D. 70. The fierce resistance of Jerusalemites would result in starvation. Mothers would eat their babies. As opposition crumbled, Jews would be massacred by the Romans. Victims would be hung on crosses till no more trees could be found. Temple and city would be burned. The city would be dug up and leveled. So vivid was Jesus' prophecy that some Bible critics wrongly claim Luke's account must have been written after A.D. 70.

Jesus weeps over villages, towns, and cities today if they are forgetting the voice of the prophets and the Gospel of the apostles. French artist Paul Flandrin in his painting *Christ Mourning Over the City*, depicts a metropolitan city, not Jerusalem, with crowded tenements in the foreground, a dark cathedral looming in the background, unlit to symbolize the spiritual darkness engulfing the city. Midst the splendor lurk poverty, degradation, and neglect.

Cities are merely concentrated centers of human attitudes toward Him. Christ laments over Chicago, New York, London, Paris, Tokyo, and others. He sees every soul who walks therein. He knows every person, respected or ruined. Poet George Santa writes:

> We are the men of the city street,
> We are the men whose footsteps beat
> Weary marches through empty years
> Dreary tempos to falling tears,
> Men whose souls are damned by sin,
> Men whose hearts are dead within,
> Broken bodies—we dream of death
> And joy in Life's receding breath. . . .
> Broken souls, and the yawning grave
> Holds more terrors than e'er it gave
> Of respite to our motley lot;
> We are the men that Life forgot.

Then comes the answer from the weeping Christ:
> I am the Christ of the city street,
> I walk its miles with bleeding feet,
> I see the men whose lives are spent
> In deepest night and banishment
> From all that human hearts hold dear,
> I see the ghosts of men walk here.
> I see their faces gaunt and thin,
> The sinful hearts I long to win,
> I know their burdens, feel their pain,
> And yearn to turn their loss to gain;
> I note the falter in their tread,
> I see the pallor of the dead
> Upon their faces, and I stand
> To offer them My nail-scarred hand,
> But now I weep, for even they
> Sneer mockingly and turn away. . . .
> Yes, of this city I'm a part—
> I walk its streets with bleeding heart.

We need Christ's heart of sorrow to see people who haven't received Christ as Saviour as blind and headed for certain judgment. Often we fail to realize that well-dressed, well-fed, prosperous people are just as lost and doomed as derelicts. Do we visualize people outside of Christ as headed for eternal punishment?

One Sunday afternoon in Biloxi, Mississippi, an hour before the final service of an area-wide evangelistic crusade, a denominational leader lamented the spiritual indifference of people along the Gulf Coast. Standing in front of the stadium where the crusade had been held, with tears in his eyes he exclaimed. "How long will God be patient with these people? One of these days His judgment will let a hurricane come down this coast and destroy this place!"

Two weeks later, almost to the very hour, Hurricane Camille struck, devastating the Gulf Coast, wiping out gambling dens and night spots. The Biloxi town fathers, worried over the stadium turf, had almost withheld permission for its use as the crusade site. When the storm subsided, tons of debris had washed inland, filling the stadium and totally ripping up the turf.

How strange we weep so easily over fictional characters, but fail to shed a tear over real-life tragedy. In one soap opera the heroine was unwittingly about to marry a villain. The television station was so besieged with threats to boycott the sponsor's product if the two characters married that the wedding never came off. Likely, some of the protestors knew of young folks in real life about to make tragic decisions, for whom they had little concern.

Jesus' tears over Jerusalem did not flow in vain. Multitudes believed on Him, well over 5,000 (Acts 4:4; 5:14). Their blindness had been removed. Christ's eyes had been darkened with tears that their eyes might be enlightened with the truth.

Paul's great heaviness and continual sorrow must often have overflowed from heart to eyes, as he wished himself accursed from Christ for his brethren, his kinsmen according to the flesh (Rom. 9:2-3). In his three-year stay in Ephesus he "ceased not to warn every one night and day with tears" (Acts 20:31).

It was written of the famous evangelist, George Whitefield, that the people could not dislike the man who wept so much over their souls. An English clergyman, who at first criticized D. L. Moody, later changed his opinion after hearing the evangelist preach on several occasions. The clergyman saw that Moody could never speak of a lost soul without tears in his eyes.

The psalmist promised, "They that sow in tears shall reap in joy. He that goeth forth and weepeth, bearing precious seed, shall doubtless come again with rejoicing, bringing his sheaves with him" (Ps. 126:5-6).

In the Garden

All recorded instances of our Lord's weeping took place toward the end of His ministry. Sorrow at Lazarus' grave occurred in the final weeks. Tears were shed over Jerusalem on Palm Sunday. Then the night of Jesus' arrest, the third incident happened.

After observing the Passover and instituting the Lord's Supper, Jesus and the 11 crossed the Brook Kidron and entered the Garden of Gethsemane, a small, quiet retreat at the foot of the Mount of

Olives, which Jesus often visited. The place was well-known to Judas, who at that very moment was about to lead a band of soldiers there to arrest Jesus.

Leaving eight disciples at the outer edge, but craving human fellowship, Jesus took the inner circle of Peter, James, and John a little farther. Asking them to watch with Him, He proceeded a stone's throw beyond. Then He fell forward to the ground, affording one of the most mysterious scenes ever recorded.

Before Him lay the ordeal of arrest, trial, scourging, and the cross—a death reserved for criminals, aliens, and slaves. Matthew says He began to be exceedingly sorrowful (26:38). Mark quotes Jesus, "My soul is overwhelmed with sorrow to the point of death" (14:34, NIV). Dr. Luke mentions that He sweat as it were great drops of blood (22:44). Though none of the writers say specifically that He wept, the excessive emotion of sweating blood would likely indicate the prior existence of tears.

The writer of the Book of Hebrews, undoubtedly referring to the Gethsemane experience, clearly speaks of weeping. "Who in the days of His flesh, when He had offered up prayers and supplications with strong crying and tears unto Him that was able to save Him from death, and was heard in that He feared; though He were a Son, yet learned He obedience by the things which He suffered" (Heb. 5:7-8).

Overwhelmed at the contents of the cup of iniquity which He had volunteered to drink, He wrestled in prayer—agonizing, crying loudly, sweating blood. Would it be possible for this cup to pass from Him? If not, He submitted, "Not My will, but Thine be done" (Luke 22:42).

Why did Jesus weep so vehemently? Was He not beginning to see more clearly the horribleness of sin? He who knew no sin was about to be made sin for us, the sin-bearer substitute accepted by divine justice to bear the divine wrath that we might never bear it. Because of the sinfulness of sin—its guilt, shame, and penalty—He wept.

Modern theories try to minimize the awfulness of sin. Sin has been declared a remnant of our animal nature, an inferiority complex, an error of mortal mind, a cultural lag, an antisocial behavior, or a limitation of being. But to find out how loathsome sin is, just watch the Saviour under the gnarled and knotted olive trees in Gethsemane, as He prays, weeps, and sweats.

In a dream a man saw Christ being scourged. As the tormentor swished the whip through the air, striking with its little bits of pointed metal into the victim's back, the man could stand it no longer. Running forward, he yelled, "Stop!" But on reaching the tormentor and looking into his face, to his horror he saw himself.

Perhaps, if in a moment of temptation we could recall it was our iniquity that helped make Jesus weep, this would enable us to gain the victory. That unkind word, nasty deed, unfaithfulness to our mate, insidious slander, malicious envy, hate, racial prejudice, social snobbery, cheating on our income tax, insolent disobedience to parents, excessive love of material things—all helped make Christ shed tears in the Garden.

How easy it is for us to become hardened to increasing violence, pornography, immorality, and injustice. We need a developing sensitivity to sin, like the Apostle Paul, who in mid-career called himself an apostle (1 Cor. 9:1), later termed himself the least of all saints (Eph. 3:8), then in one of his last epistles, styled himself the chief of sinners (2 Tim. 1:15). As he grew in grace and conformity to the image of Christ, he could see more clearly the exceeding sinfulness of sin.

We must never treat sin lightly. We should shed some tears over our own shortcomings, but also mourn the transgressions of others, saying with the psalmist, "Rivers of waters run down mine eyes, because they keep not Thy law" (Ps. 119:136).

May God grant us hearts like Christ's that can overflow in times of sorrow, over blind and condemned souls, and over the reality of sin.

2
The Patience
of Jesus

Not long ago a West German sculptor finished four full-size wax models from which the large bronze doors for the western facade of Washington's National Cathedral will be cast. Thirty-five years ago, during World War II, this sculptor, while a prisoner-of-war in an American Army camp in Italy, used razor blades to carve his first works from ammunition box scraps.

The Lord frequently keeps His children in obscurity while they develop their talents, then brings them into the open when fully prepared. John the Baptist lived in the wilderness till the day God directed him to begin preaching repentance up and down the Jordan valley.

Likewise, the Lord Jesus was hidden behind the scenes for 30 years before God's signal propelled Him on His public ministry.

Patience in Postponement

A nervous deacon, pacing the floor, was asked by a friend the reason for his frenzy. Came the answer, "My problem is—I'm in a hurry—and God isn't!"

In contrast to human impatience stands the patience of Christ. Though His public life extended only three years, He underwent 30 years of preparation.

At 12, His emerging messianic consciousness enabled Him to

converse intelligently with learned doctors in the temple. He was "sitting in the midst of the doctors, both hearing them, and asking them questions. And all that heard Him were astonished at His understanding and answers" (Luke 2:46-47). In His teens and twenties, His sensitive nature must have noticed the hollow hypocrisy of the religious leaders. They were so concerned about outward ceremony, borders on their cloaks, and upper seats at dinners, yet so void of concern for the outcasts, lost, and lonely.

Also as a young man, Jesus must have been moved with compassion on the hungry, sick, and demon-possessed. He must have longed to emerge on His public mission to preach the truth and heal the sick.

But he waited, and waited, and waited till He was 30 years old. Did the responsibility of His home in Nazareth require His oversight all those years? Or was He conscious of His need for long years of preparation? Whatever the reason, His waiting displayed patience.

After the Lord did commence His public ministry, He must have longed for the completion of His task. But He had to wait long months till He even told His disciples that He would go to the cross, die, and rise the third day.

Enemies plotted His death prematurely. Attempts were made on His life. Opponents took up stones to cast at Him. His townfolk tried to push Him over a hill. Soldiers, sent to arrest Him, returned empty-handed. His unbelieving brothers taunted Him to open declaration. Jesus said, "My time is not yet come" (John 7:6).

With calm deliberation He waited for the appointed hour. On the cross He died at the predetermined moment, not a second early or late. No man took His life from Him, but He gave up the ghost, committing His Spirit into His Father's hand (Luke 23:46). This was patience supreme.

He was never in a hurry, never flustered, always poised and calm of spirit. Someone referred to His pace as the "gait of Galilee." An old farmer had a woodpile that needed sawing. Because his saw was dull, he had a dreadful time making it go at all. When a neighbor suggested getting the saw sharpened, the farmer retorted, "Don't bother me. I've got enough to do to saw that pile of wood without stopping to sharpen the saw." Those who follow the poised pace of Jesus must have the patience to take time for meditation in the Word, prayer, and relaxation, else they will find their labor difficult, discouraging, and barren.

When I finished Bible school, I wanted to become a pastor. But no offers came. Then when I went to college, I thought sure I would receive a call to become student pastor to some church. Still no invitation came. Then I went to seminary. Not till my final year was I called to the pastorate of a church.

Are you waiting for some cherished, God-given dream to come true? Sometimes in the divine schedule, slow is fast. Delays are not denials. No letter to heaven goes unanswered, but God does have a file marked "pending."

Patience in Training the Twelve

The prime purpose for Jesus' coming to earth was to pay the penalty for our sins. But how would the good news of forgiveness through His death and resurrection become known to the people of His day, and through time to countless generations? His plan was to have apostles carry his message to the nations of the world. Thus, a major task of Jesus' ministry was the training of the Twelve.

Since these men would have to be more than casual acquaintances, He called them "that they should be with Him" (Mark 3:14). He wanted them to live continuously in the atmosphere of His life, and to be permeated with His influence. So, He taught them day by day. But how slowly they learned. How patient He was with them.

Many times the disciples were within earshot of Jesus as He was praying. Though He had certain things He wished to teach them in that area, He waited till they took the initiative by asking, "Lord, teach us to pray" (Luke 11:1).

Always present to hear His words and see His miracles, the Twelve didn't always understand. After the parable of the sower was given publicly, the disciples asked Him what the parable might mean (Mark 4:10). Patiently He explained it in detail. In fact, more space seems devoted to the private explanation than to the public utterance. Other occasions of this same practice are recorded in Matthew 13:36ff; 15:15ff; and Luke 12:22ff.

The same night after feeding the 5,000 Jesus came walking on the water to the storm-tossed disciples whom He had dispatched to cross the Sea of Galilee. At first they were terrified by His presence, but calmed down when He said, "Be of good cheer: it is I; be not afraid." They were amazed at the miracle of His walking on water. How soon they had forgotten the lesson of the feeding of the 5,000 just a few hours before. Mark concludes, "For they considered not the miracle of the loaves: for their heart was hardened" (Mark 6:50-52).

Jesus had proven His power by feeding 5,000 with 12 basketfuls to spare. But when a similar situation arose again, this time 4,000 going with little to eat for three days, the disciples were guilty of unbelief. For when Jesus suggested the need to feed the multitude, the Twelve seem to have completely forgotten the former miracle. So incredible seems their stupidity that some doubting commentators claim that the writer must have borrowed some of the narrative from the previous story. With patience Jesus performed another miracle, this time with seven baskets of food left over (Mark 8:1ff).

When the disciples failed to understand His warning against the leaven of the Pharisees and of Herod, He rebuked them, "Perceive ye not yet, neither understand? Have ye your heart yet hardened? Having eyes, see ye not? And having ears, hear ye not? And do ye not remember?" (vv. 17-18)

How discouraging to Jesus when the inner three disciples, Peter, James, and John, fell asleep both on the Mount of Transfiguration and in Gethsemane (Luke 9:32; Matt. 26:40ff). How badly He must have felt when all denied Him, forsook Him, and fled.

Two major lessons the disciples repeatedly failed to learn during Jesus' public ministry were those of humility and His resurrection.

First, humility. How slow they were to understand, frequently arguing over who would be the greatest in the coming kingdom. Once, Jesus put a child in their midst, exhorting them to childlike humility (Mark 9:34-37).

But the disciples didn't learn the lesson. They continued to argue among themselves about who would be chief executive in the kingdom. James and John even aspired through their mother's intercession to the two top seats.

The Lord answered that though heathen men sought to land the number one spot, His followers were to be the opposite. "Whosoever will be great among you, shall be your minister; and whosoever of you will be chiefest, shall be servant of all." Then to offset the arrogant attitude of His disciples He introduced the lowliness of His own service, "For even the Son of man came not to be ministered unto, but to minister, and to give His life a ransom for many" (Mark 10:35-45).

But the disciples still failed to practice humility. In fact, during the Passover supper, with the Saviour's cross less than 24 hours away, the reclining apostles inappropriately fought among themselves about who should rank highest in the coming kingdom. Again our Lord patiently admonished them, asking "whether is greater, he that sitteth at meat, or he that serveth? Is not he that sitteth at meat?" Then came the clincher, "I am among you as he that serveth" (Luke 22:26-27).

At this point, according to some scholars, Jesus rose to do a servant's chore. Common courtesy called for a host to wash his guests' feet. Because the Upper Room was borrowed, no servant was present to take care of the usual ablutions. But basin and towel had been thoughtfully provided. Who would do the menial task?

With the atmosphere charged with feverish ambition, no aspiring leader was about to kneel before his subjects. Each regarded the task too demeaning. Then, amazingly, Jesus picked up the basin and towel. The Lord of Glory chose the servant's place, taking the soiled feet in His own hands. Completing the round, he exhorted humility on the basis of His example, "If I then, your Lord and Master, have washed your feet; ye also ought to wash one another's feet. For I have given you an example, that ye should do as I have done to you" (John 13:14-15). Jesus was patient right to the end.

Another major truth Jesus had difficulty in getting across to the disciples had to do with His death and resurrection. The first time He spoke of His death plainly to the Twelve, Peter rebuked Him for it. Many times before His arrest He foretold His sufferings, death, and resurrection. Earlier references may have been veiled such as, "Destroy this temple, and in three days I will raise it up" (John 2:19). But later predictions were unequivocally clear (Mark

9:31-32; 10:32-34). Both these statements contain a third-day resurrection. Whenever He uttered such prophecies, they did not understand the saying (Luke 9:45).

When the resurrection did take place, the disciples didn't believe it at first. The news seemed like an idle tale. On the other hand, His enemies so believed the saying that they requested the sealing of the tomb by Roman authorities.

The resurrected Christ gently chided His followers for their lack of understanding. He reproached the Emmaus disciples, "O fools, and slow of heart to believe all that the prophets have spoken" (Luke 24:25). Then He explained how Moses and the prophets predicted the events of the passion. Later the same evening He explained the same Scriptures to the 10 in the Upper Room. He was patience personified.

While preparing the material for this chapter, I had to make a pastoral call at a nearby hospital. Approaching a toll booth on the way, I found myself in line behind a car which had stalled. I fumed and fretted. Then it suddenly dawned on me that I had just left my office, where I had been meditating on the patience of Christ, and that I wasn't practicing it.

How often we say, "I told you once, do I have to tell you again?" Or, "Speed it up." Or, "You never get it right. I always have to tell you how to do it." The warm, caring heart of Jesus reminds us to patiently put up with imperfect people.

How easy to lose patience with an erring brother. People irritate us because they don't catch on to our instructions as soon as we would like them to. Paul urged Timothy to exhort "with all the patience that the work of teaching requires" (2 Tim. 4:2, NEB). He also urged us to "encourage the faint-hearted, help the weak, be patient with them all" (1 Thes. 5:14, RSV).

Robert Shurbet was born in 1922, a spastic. Given up for dead at first, but then revived, he learned later that doctors pessimistically predicted only a few days of life for him. However, at two years he was still hanging on. His parents were told that since his legs were crossed, he would never walk—but just exist as a helpless bundle of humanity.

Shurbet wrote, "My mother was determined that I should walk so she worked faithfully with me, exercising the various parts of my body. My chief exercises were those that would help uncross my legs. My mother's patient efforts were rewarded. At five, I could take a few hesitant steps alone. By my sixth birthday, I could feed myself. At nine I had about the same physical control of myself as an 18-month-old baby.

"Againt the wishes of the principal I started to school at eight. I had to be carried there every day by my parents, then entrusted to the care of teachers for the rest of the day. No one, except members of my family, could understand a word I said. I could not do many things other children did, like drawing, cutting out pictures, or moving around the room without the aid of a teacher or classmate. Most of the children were kind to me, but sometimes I could be knocked down on purpose in a crowded hallway.

"Though physically handicapped, I was mentally capable. By the time I reached fifth grade I could walk the three blocks to school when accompanied by a friend. Later we moved to the country where I had to walk a whole mile to school every day. How surprised were those who had predicted I would never walk!

"For two years during junior high school I studied at a school for spastics. I learned to walk better, use my hands, and speak much plainer. The two accomplishments of which I am most proud are learning to speak so everyone could understand everything I said and learning to use a fork. These achievements represented 18 years of concentrated effort with the help of patient people.

"In my senior year of high school, I won second place in a speech contest of 40 entrants. I finished in the upper 10 percent of my class. But I could not write legibly, so did all my writing on a typewriter, a very awkward, tiring process.

"I went to college, later married against the wishes of both sets of parents who thought that two handicapped people couldn't make it. [Shurbet's wife had cerebral palsy.] But we did. We both secured jobs teaching cerebral palsied children.

"Feeling the call of God to the ministry, I took an assignment in a little church. But soon after, though parishioners told me I preached excellent sermons, they admitted embarrassment at having a 'crippled' preacher, and dismissed me.

"I then attended and graduated from Southeastern Bible College in Birmingham, Alabama. I became a full-time instructor there, and accepted a part-time pastorate. My life verse was Philippians 4:13, 'I can do all things through Christ which strengtheneth me.' The Lord enabled me to do many 'impossible' things. I wrote inspirational articles for rural newspapers in areas where I pastored churches, and for denominational periodicals. I was ordained, and pastored a full-time church in suburban Birmingham, and also served as moderator of the Birmingham Presbytery." (This quote was taken from letters written by Robert Shurbet.)

Robert died at 36. His amazing accomplishments in the face of such seemingly insurmountable odds would never have been realized apart from the patient instruction of parents, teachers, and friends.

Patient Under Provocation of Opponents

The scribes and Pharisees repeatedly tried to entrap Jesus in His speech, especially during His final week (Luke 11:53-54; Matt. 22:15ff).

Insults increased during the final 24 hours of His life. When the yelling mob came to arrest Him in the garden, He could have summoned thousands of angels to wipe out the motley crowd, but He let them take Him. He didn't revile Judas as he committed his treacherous deed. Rather, He allowed Judas to kiss Him, even calling the traitor, "Friend" (Matt. 26:50). When Peter cut off the ear of the high priest's servant, Malchus, Jesus restored the dismembered part.

Accused by false witnesses before Caiaphas and the Sanhedrin, "He held His peace" (Mark 14:61).

When the chief priests, scribes, and elders blasphemed, mocked, buffeted, blindfolded, and slapped Him, sneering, "Prophesy, who is it that smote Thee?" He remained patient (Luke 22:63-65).

Before Pilate's tribunal, denounced by the chief priests and elders, He maintained His undisturbed demeanor. He answered nothing, except when ordered to respond under oath.

Shunted off to Herod because He came under his jurisdiction, and mockingly dressed up in make-believe royal robes, He took it sweetly (Luke 23:9-11).

Pilate ordered Jesus scourged. The cruel whip lashed His back, cutting deeply and perhaps swishing around to gash His front. The soldiers scoffingly placed a crown of thorns on His brow, outfitted Him in a scarlet garment, put a reed in His hand as a make-believe scepter, bowed as if to worship, and saluted Him "King of the Jews" (Matt. 27:27-31). Then they spat on His face, wrenched the reed from His hand, smote Him on the head, pulled off the robe, and put His own raiment back on. But He never complained.

Lifted up on the cross, He became an object of sarcasm. Passersby wagged their heads, "You said You could rebuild the temple in three days." Rulers, chief priests, scribes, and elders derided Him, "He saved others: Himself He cannot save. Come down from the cross and we will believe you" (Mark 15:29-32). The soldiers jeered. At first both thieves cast the same scoffings in His face. But all through the six hours of the cross, not a cry of bitterness broke the stillness. Instead, "Father, forgive them; for they know not what they do" (Luke 23:34).

How humiliating for the Lord of glory to take such abuse from sinful, loathsome creatures. Thomas a Kempis in his *Imitation of Christ* says, "He deserves not the name of patient who is only willing to suffer as much as he thinks proper, and from whom he pleases. The truly patient man asks not from whom he suffers, his superior, his equal, or his inferior; whether from a good and holy man, or one who is perverse and unworthy. But from whomsoever, how muchsoever, or how oftensoever wrong is done him, he accepts it all as from the hand of God, and counts it gain."

A seminary student worked for a construction company during his summer vacation. When the foreman learned that his new crew member was a local preacher's son, he was determined to break him. That summer he cursed the lad, criticized his work without grounds, made him tear out a job and do it over for no reason, and even kicked him on more than one occasion.

Many days the boy came home, saying, "Dad, I don't think I can take another day." His father would pray with him and encourage him to stick it out. He did.

A few months later, guess who walked in the church door to visit a service? Later that same foreman professed Christ.

The cross stands out not only as an act of unique atonement, but also as an example of patience under suffering. The Lord certainly practiced what He preached in warning His disciples of coming persecution, "In your patience possess ye your souls" (21:19).

3
The Anger
of Jesus

"Angry Motorist Helps Tame Parkway" headlined a story in an eastern paper. Motorists heading northbound on the Hutchinson River Parkway a few miles out of New York City used to find their view of the roadway ahead completely blocked by the crest of a hill. This lack of "sight distance" resulted in 28 rear-end collisions and six injuries over a span of 30 months.

One of these accidents involved a commercial airline pilot. "I never had an accident before and I think I have good reflexes. But though I had reduced my speed to 20 miles per hour as I approached the crest, I suddenly discovered a back up of cars. I applied the brakes but slammed into the back of a car, which in turn hit another vehicle. Though my car sustained $1,800 worth of damages, what incensed me most was the official indifference to the dangerous situation—even after two similar crashes at the same spot within minutes of my accident. The parkway police didn't seem to take the situation very seriously."

In anger this pilot contacted the AAA whose subsequent conferences with parkway authorities resulted in the installation of an overhead sign, "Cars Stopped Ahead." Sensors imbedded in the roadway now activate the warning sign when traffic has slowed dangerously. Flashing on and off in bright red letters, these three words alert motorists to potential danger ahead. The article commented, "The safety device owes its existence to an irate motorist." Anger helped correct a dangerous situation.

Jesus sometimes became angry. This surprises many people. Jesus angry? How could that be? Was He not love incarnate? Was He not tender with the worst of humans?

But the same word for *anger* in the lists of sins in Ephesians 4:31 and Colossians 3:8 describes how Jesus reacted to the unfeeling Pharisees in the Capernaum synagogue. He "looked round about on them with anger" (Mark 3:5). How could Jesus maintain His sinlessness when He became angry?

Perhaps too often we have emphasized the love of God at the expense of His justice. God has been depicted as a wishy-washy, easily humored old granddaddy who sits in a divine rocking chair, winking at sin and condoning evil. We forget that the God of the Bible, though slow to anger, can reach the limit of His patience. The same God who saved Noah's family sent the flood that destroyed mankind. The same God who saved Lot and his daughters from destruction also rained down fire and brimstone on Sodom.

So it's not surprising to find the tenderness of Christ balanced by His toughness. Not only is He the Lamb, but also the Lion of the Tribe of Judah. Not only is He a rock in which people may find refuge, but also a stone which, falling on the ungodly, grinds them to powder. The returning Christ will lead the armies of heaven as "He treadeth the winepress of the fierceness and wrath of Almighty God" (Rev. 19:15). Though the Gospels record His mildness, His scorn was often as fierce as lightning.

Jesus' Anger Was Sinless

Anger is a devastating sin. It has terminated friendships, divided homes, led to violence, and wreaked havoc. It victimized Cain, Moses, and a host of Bible characters. The early church fathers counted it among the seven deadly sins.

Psychologically we describe anger as a surge of emotion that rises within us when something blocks our way. Adrenalin flows into the bloodstream. Muscles tense. Pulse speeds. A force within rises to a crescendo.

Many people handle anger in one of two opposite ways, both of which are wrong: unbridled expression or firm repression. If unchecked, release comes in shrill shouting, blowing our top, even lashing out in a tornado of rage. On the other extreme, many learn to cap their seething volcano by holding a grudge, acting grumpy, uttering a caustic remark, seething with longtime resentment, giving the silent treatment, or wallowing in self-pity. In either case, whether expressed or repressed, this kind of anger is sinful. Paul lists anger as a work of the flesh (Gal. 5:20). Guilt feelings reinforce biblical condemnation.

But anger isn't always sinful. God has so created us that indignation can be a valuable force in life. A moderate course between the two extremes of expression and repression is possible. When hampered by frustrating circumstances, we find an angry reaction instinctively starting to work in us; we should mobilize our anger to respond in a positive way.

However, we must always be wary of anger. I readily admit—and wouldn't most of us—that when my blood begins to boil over some frustrating situation, more often than not my ire is mixed with unholy elements. But wrath is not necessarily wrong. Jesus spoke of anger against a brother *without cause,* intimating that some anger may have justification (Matt. 5:22). Paul wrote, "Be ye angry, and sin not" (Eph. 4:26). This permissive imperative does not command us to blow our stack, but allows us anger on certain occasions. So that we don't let our anger lead to sin, Paul added, "Let not the sun go down upon your wrath" (v. 26). Anger swings into sin when it bursts out of control, explodes in profanity, or leads to hate, dissension, or violence (Prov. 16:32; Matt. 5:22; Gal. 5:20; Col. 3:8; Eph. 4:31).

James' command to be slow to anger indicates that controlled anger can be righteously expressed (James 1:19). Anger is sinless when it doesn't stem from personal pique, is directed against wrong, and is expressed in a positive fashion. Let's see how Jesus' anger filled all these qualifications.

His Anger Never Personally Motivated

Jesus' anger never stemmed from personal resentment. In contrast, our wrath is usually motivated by self-interest. Though we may pretend some noble motive, the bottom line indicates personal resentment at some real or imaginary slight. It is wounded vanity, because our pride, position, possession, or performance has been attacked. Some affront has been dealt our egos, causing the old nature to flare up.

Too often our anger is fired up when others snub, slander, or annoy *us*. When they differ with *us*. When they hurt *our* feelings, criticize *our* children, impugn *our* motives, usurp *our* place in the line, or insult *our* sensitivity. Much of our anger is spiteful, because we conclude others have given *us* the raw end of the deal.

But Jesus never spoke one word of indignation when personally mistreated. When reviled, He reviled not again. When they spat in His face, pressed a cruel crown of thorns into His Holy brow, and nailed Him to the cross, no expression of personal irritation nor cry of revenge crossed His lips. Think who He was—the image of the invisible God, the brightness of the Father's glory, the express image of His Person, Lord of heaven and earth who upheld all things by the word of His power—yet no sigh of animosity escaped His mouth.

When Jesus *did* get angry, it was never for any wrong done to Him as an individual. He didn't burn with the unholy heat of passion, but with the white fervor of His purity. His anger was never subjective, due to His own injured feelings, but objective because another had been obstructed, damaged, or prevented from realizing his best potential.

His Anger Directed Against Wrong

The event that motivated the career of the illustrious English emancipator, Lord Shaftesbury, occurred when he was 14. One day he heard drunken singing and loud yelling on a side street. As the noisy party neared the corner, he was horrified to see several intoxicated men carrying a rough, homemade coffin, containing the corpse of one of their derelict friends. Staggering, they lost their balance, letting the box fall and break partly open. The pallbearers broke out in foul, blasphemous language. The shocked teenager stood transfixed as the bizzare funeral procession stumbled by. In anger he exclaimed, "Can this be allowed to happen simply because the man was poor?" Before the boisterous song faded in the distance, he vowed he would devote his life to pleading the cause of the poor and friendless.

Indignation, to be sinless, must be properly directed. Though Christ did not return insults done to Him as a person, He did resent people and practices that barred others from the happy life He offered. In fact, He was pitiless to those that blocked the abundant life. He proved that it is possible to love the good but still get mad at evil.

Christian character is displayed by what makes us angry. Too often we get angry when things don't go our way. But Christ became irate when others were injured. Let's look at the things that made Him mad.

He was angry at the hard-heartedness and hypocrisy of the Pharisees. People usually act their sweetest in church. But one day in a house of worship Jesus' eyes blazed with anger. The Pharisees, pushing forth a man with a withered hand, perhaps deliberately planted in the crowd, waited hawk-eyed to see if Jesus would "break the Sabbath." Man-made law said it was improper to heal on that day. Jesus asked, "Is it lawful to do good on the Sabbath?" He knew the Pharisees did not really care about the withered hand, but were concerned over their religious rules. Indignant at their preverted sense of values, which put ritual above human welfare, Jesus "looked around about on them with anger, being grieved for the hardness of their hearts." Then He healed the man (Mark 3:1-5).

Matthew 23 contains an eight-fold woe blasting the scribes and Pharisees for disgusting inconsistency between their lofty religious profession and their low irreligious practice. They burdened others with strict rules which they didn't keep themselves. They were exceedingly scrupulous about outward matters, but grossly deficient in inward graces like humility, sincerity, honesty, justice, mercy, faith, and purity. By majoring in the minors, the Pharisees de-emphasized the great virtues so necessary for Christian living.

While acting so piously, they cheated widows out of property. By the trick of tradition they evaded their obligation to care for their aged parents. On these hypocrites Christ poured out the vials of His invectives, calling them "blind guides" (Matt. 23:16), "whited sepulchres" (v. 27), "serpents" (v. 33), "generations of vipers" (v. 33). With eyes flashing, He warned, "How can ye escape the damnation of hell?" (v. 33). He could not have used stronger language. Behind His scathing denunciation was this complaint, "Ye shut up the kingdom of heaven against men: for ye neither go in yourselves, neither suffer ye them that are entering to go in" (v. 13). Their hardheartedness and hypocrisy kept people from realizing God's best in this world and in the world to come.

Their culminating atrocity occurred on the morning of the crucifixion when they led Jesus to Pilate's judgment hall. However, they themselves did not go in, lest they should be defiled and unable to eat the Passover (John 18:28). So particular about a ceremonial law, yet they could engineer an innocent man's execution.

The Saviour was most gracious to sinners who acknowledged their wrong and sought His forgiveness. But for religious hypocrites who mistreated fellow humans and blocked them from entrance to the kingdom, He had only His flaming scorn.

He was angry at the money changers in the temple. In Jesus' day when worshipers brought sacrifices to the temple, the sacrifices were usually found unacceptable by the priests. This would force the worshiper to buy an acceptable animal from the priest, who had a thriving business operating within the confines of the temple, selling sheep raised on the hills of Bethlehem.

The outer court had become a dirty, smelly, roaring market with the deafening din of sellers hawking their wares, the bleating of sheep, the cackling of caged birds, and the noise of bargaining, where the honest worshiper would find only confusion and blasphemy.

Long before, the temple had ceased to be a place of prayer and worship and had become a money-making bazaar that provided lucrative income for "pious" priests. Knowing this, the Lord Jesus cleansed the temple twice in His ministry, once at the beginning and again at the end.

Making a scourge of small cords, Jesus strode into the temple. His eyes ablaze with anger, He dumped the money bags on the floor, overturned tables, drove out the cattle, freed the cooped birds, and shouted at the evildoers who fled before His fury, "Take these things hence. . . . My house shall be called the house of prayer; but ye have made it a den of thieves (John 2:16; Matt. 21:13).

Many a church today has turned away from its primary purposes. No longer is there the worship of the triune God, the teaching of the Word, the fellowship of saints, the service of others, and the winning of the lost. Beautiful edifices do not make a church. Perhaps we need parishioners who will rise up in righteous anger and cleanse their temples.

He was angry when little children were kept from Him. When mothers brought their little ones to Jesus to bless, the disciples rebuked them, thinking their Master was too busy. "Can't you see how tired the Master is? Don't bother Him with such nonsense" (see Mark 10:13). But Jesus seeing what was happening, was moved with indignation and said, "Suffer the little children to come unto Me, and forbid them not: for of such is the kingdom of God" (v. 14). Then He lifted the babies in His arms, and blessed them.

One of Jesus' harshest warnings is reserved for those who would offend children. "Whoso shall offend one of these little ones which believe in Me, it were better for him that a millstone were hanged about his neck, and that he were drowned in the depth of the sea" (Matt. 18:6).

The dope-peddler who entices children into taking drugs, then succeeds in hooking those children into regular usage faces the wrath of Christ. The moviemaker who enlists children into playing pornographic parts in X-rated movies is headed for certain judgment.

The Washington Post recently reported that several thousand children under 12 have been sold by parents in Thailand and recruited for work in factories in Bangkok. These children work 12 hours a day, seven days a week with no holidays, unable to leave the factory except on rare occasions, and only under escort.

Such a report horrifies us. But we should not blind ourselves to situations in our homes and communities where children are exploited or mistreated. Warned Jesus, "Take heed that ye despise not one of these little ones" (v. 10).

He was angry at death. Death, a terrible enemy, has a key to every country, every street, every home. It cares nothing for our plans.

Sometimes the young die before the old, and the strong before the weak. What sorrow death causes to the mother who loses her little child, to the wife bereft of her husband, to the boy frustrated at the loss of his dad.

When Jesus returned to Bethany and found Martha and Mary mourning the loss of their brother Lazarus, He "groaned in the spirit" (John 11:33). The same verb is used five verses later when in a few moments, coming to the grave, He was "groaning in himself" (v. 38). In classical Greek this verb *groan* was used in the sense of hot anger. It means to snort, express indignation. Seeing the many mourners with their tears of despair, Jesus advanced toward the grave of Lazarus with indignant emotion. Death had occasioned His holy wrath. It had robbed them and Him of their loved one. Inwardly angry, He may have said to Himself, "I'll take revenge against the ravages of death when I get the chance."

In all these instances of Jesus' anger, He was aroused not by insults or injuries heaped on Him, but by people or activities which frustrated His purposes of benevolence to the human race.

Anger Expressed Constructively

In the early days of movies when western thrillers were first shown in ranch towns, cowboys came in from miles around to watch the villain as he held up banks, shot up the town, and held the pretty heroine at his mercy. Often the cowboys became so angry that they pulled their guns and shot at the villain on the screen. They failed to realize that they damaged the movie-house furniture and missed the villain completely. More recently some people have started throwing bricks at their television sets in disgust at the violence. Because repairs are so costly, one ingenius company began making rubber bricks.

Aristotle in his Ethics (IV, 5, 7) observed that people are often angry for the wrong reasons, in a wrong way, with the wrong folk, and for the wrong length of time. But it is possible to harness anger in a positive way. Someone quipped, "We need to know how to be good—and mad."

As earlier noted, we should avoid the two extremes in dealing with anger. Rather than throwing a tantrum or bottling our anger within, we should channel this force constructively into patience, steadfastness, and determination to bring about a positive change. Wrath must not only oppose, but propose.

Martin Luther said that he never worked better than when inspired by anger. "When I am angry I can write, pray, and preach well; for then my whole temperament is quickened, my understanding sharpened, and all mundane vexations and temptations depart." Another preacher said, "Usually I weigh 120 pounds; when I'm mad, I weigh a ton." An officer who won the Congressional Medal of Honor by waging a one-man war against hopeless odds, asked to explain how he did it, replied "I just got mad."

The Lord Jesus put His anger to constructive purposes. Indignant at the Pharisees for their hardhearted objection to healing a man on the Sabbath, Jesus restored his withered hand. Aroused at the desecration of the temple, He cleansed it. Peeved at the disciples for keeping infants from Him, He took the babies in His arms and blessed them. Incensed at the power of death which had taken His friend, Lazarus, He vowed to break its power, and did so by His resurrection.

English jails were vile, filthy, disease-ridden holes till John Howard and his followers got angry, and were instrumental in effecting major prison reforms. Hospitals were horrible till Florence Nightingale lost her cool. This angel of mercy was a high-tempered woman who hounded government officials into providing decent care for the wounded. Lord Shaftesbury, mentioned earlier, angry at the degradation and exploitation of the young, poor, and underprivileged in England, pushed strong measures through English Parliament that humanized conditions in mines and factories throughout the land.

In the final analysis Christian anger is but the reverse side of Christian love. Because every person is immeasurably precious in God's sight, we should hate whatever ills prevent human beings from reaching their God-intended fullness. We should love the right so strongly that we detest evil.

Can we shut our eyes to the evils about us? In one city where a small band of aroused citizens broke the strangle-hold of racketeers, the local newspaper commented, "Any group of honest men, when they get mad enough, can drive out crime and make an awful lot of trouble for the criminals."

What about the gambling octopus, the tobacco manufacturers whose cigarettes sold in the Third World usually contain twice as much cancer-causing tar as identical brands elsewhere, the dope rings, the proliferation of pornography, and the low moral tone of many TV programs? Shouldn't these make our temperatures rise?

Not long ago (1980) an aroused evangelical community in Santa Clara County (which includes San Jose) in California, representing some 600 area churches, defeated by nearly a three-to-one margin measures which sought to give homosexuals the right to sue if denied housing, employment, or governmental services solely because of sexual preference.

After the Civil War, General Robert E. Lee was approached by the managers of the infamous Louisiana Lottery. They wanted no money from him, just the use of his name, for which they would make him rich. Unable to believe his ears, General Lee asked them to repeat their offer. Straightening up in his chair, and buttoning his old gray tunic about him, he thundered, "Gentlemen, I lost my home in the war. I lost my fortune in the war. I lost everything except my name. My name is not for sale, and if you fellows don't get out of here I'll break this crutch over your heads."

Anger is a divinely implanted emotion to arouse us to fight for the right. We need to utilize some of that passion, cleansed by divine control, and harness it to the work of God's kingdom for the elevation of human life.

4
The Compassion
of Jesus

Compassion is a word whose meaning has become very real to a family in the church where I serve as pastor. On a September Saturday afternoon in 1979, on a vacation in New England, Mike and Jan Sonnenberg and their two little children were involved in a multi-car accident when a truck plowed into a line of cars at the toll booth on Interstate Highway 95 near Hampton, New Hampshire. With several cars catching fire Mike received multiple lacerations and bad burns to his left hand, arm, and shoulder. But it was little 22-month-old Joel who suffered most severely, sustaining third degree burns over 85 percent of his body. Says Mike, "Joel looked like a war victim, entirely black. I had never seen anyone burned that much."

Father and son were rushed to different hospitals, with Joel soon transferred to the famous Shriners Burn Institute in Boston. He had lost his fingers, toes, ears, nose, eyelids, and lips. Though burns reached deep into his skull, he was spared any brain damage. But no one had ever survived after suffering such severe burns. Joel's plastic tent in the Bacterial Controlled Nursing Unit was the only one of its kind in the world.

But a year after the accident Joel, wearing a helmet, was attending Sunday School regularly, playing with toys like any active two-year-old, his body laced with skin grafts from the tiny portions

36

of his own body which did not burn off in the accident. He has already undergone some 20 separate operations.

Mike and Jan cannot say "thanks" enough for the evidences of Christian compassion that flowed to their family from the day of the accident. Originally coming from Michigan, the Sonnenbergs had no relatives or friends in New England. But strangers quickly became friends as what they call the "Christian network" went to work. On the day of the accident Jan and Jami, their then three-year-old daughter, went to Boston to the hospital but had no place to stay. A lady took Jami in for a week, freeing Jan to shuttle between her husband's and Joel's hospitals. "When she came back," says her mother, "she had no fear or trauma about the whole accident."

Jan also says, "Our church folks would contact people they knew, and they, in turn, would contact their friends. Folks drove up from the church with needed items. Park Street Church in Boston found me a place to stay. Persons we didn't know kept coming from various churches to lend support."

With immediate official action and simultaneous groundswell backing, our church established "The Sonnenberg Fund" with contributions in the thousands. Also, a group of young couples sponsored a church-wide potluck supper, spent time praying for the Sonnenbergs, and took up an offering sufficient to buy them a car. Financial, moral, and spiritual assistance was generously given by the families of Nyack College where Mike is a professor. When the Sonnenbergs took a short vacation at Camp of the Woods the following summer, the staff shared some of their hard-earned summer pay in a love gift for Joel.

Mike and Jan report, "People are praying for Joel in South America, in Africa, everywhere in the world. People have written from Oregon, Wyoming, and Florida. It's unreal!"

As a pastor, I have never witnessed such an outpouring of compassion, as it has gone out to this family who have continuously rung the praise note to their Lord and Saviour in every aspect of this accident.

Despite many widespread acts of kindness to help alleviate personal suffering and national tragedy in many places on the face of the earth, the world is basically unsympathetic. Cruelty lurks close to the surface of civilization. Much of humanity is rough and tough, calloused and cold, indifferent to the distress of fellowmen. Emotionally jaded by the staggering weight of the world's woes, and often selfishly wrapped up in our own interests, we fail to extend the needed helping hand.

Against this backdrop of unconcern stands the tender Lord Jesus Christ, of whom it was repeatedly asserted, "He was moved with compassion" (Matt. 9:36, 14:14; Mark 1:41, 6:34). Over and over again some individual or group elicited His deep-seated pity.

The word for compassion refers to the bowels or viscera. A compassionate person was one whose insides were stirred, resulting in tender affection. Compassion was a dominant trait of the Lord Jesus Christ.

His Compassion on the Hungry

The feedings of both the 5,000 and the 4,000 were motivated by compassion. In the first instance the record says Jesus "was moved with compassion toward them" (Mark 6:34). In the second case Jesus speaks, "I have compassion on the multitude, because they continue with Me now three days, and have nothing to eat: and I will not send them away fasting, lest they faint in the way" (Matt. 15:32).

In both episodes the crowds had physical hunger which they were unable to satisfy. For the 5,000 the day had worn to a close. For the 4,000 three days had elapsed without eating food, so great was their desire to be in Christ's presence. He who had felt the pangs of hunger in the wilderness during the 40 days of temptation, now had compassion on the crowd. He did not berate them for their failure to plan ahead, nor did He heed the disciples' suggestion to send the multitude away. He used His power to feed them. Notice His practicality in saving the leftovers—12 baskets full after feeding the 5,000 and 7 baskets full after feeding the 4,000.

The U.S. Presidential Commission on World Hunger recently pointed out that at least one out of every eight people on earth suffers malnutrition severe enough to shorten lifespan, stunt physical growth, and dull mental abilities. Approximately 450 million people would come under this classification. In addition, chronic undernutrition is another problem which results when people consume fewer calories and less protein than their bodies require to lead active, healthy lives. Though continuous shortages are not as spectacular as outright starvation, they steadily consume a greater toll in human life.

A Peace Corps volunteer serving in Latin America tells of a family in his village with four children and a horse. The income from use of the horse made it possible for the family to eat. One day one of the children became desperately ill. The only source for medicine was the sale of the horse, so the choice became one of either selling the horse or letting the child die. The parents reasoned that they could always have another child, but horses were expensive to come by. They kept the horse.

Dr. John Stott says that world need should appeal to our heads (so that we are informed), our mouths (so that we spread pertinent facts), our pockets (so that we give), but first of all to our hearts. He says, "When Jesus saw the multitudes hungry and leaderless, He was moved with compassion, and then fed them or taught them or both. It was compassion that aroused and directed His action, and it is compassion that we need most. We have to feel what Jesus felt—the pangs of the hungry, the alienation of the powerless, and the indignities of the wretched of the earth" ("The Just Demands of Economic Inequality," *Christianity Today*, May 23, 1980, p. 30).

The great crime of the rich man, as Jesus told the story, was his failure to respond to the pleas of Lazarus for food. The rich man's heart was not moved with pity, though he could see and hear the beggar who was at his gate every day (Luke 16:19-25).

How can Christians help today? Through the years Senator Mark Hatfield has made many suggestions such as fasting periodically, minimizing waste, limiting consumption of meat, planting home gardens, feeding scraps instead of commercial food to pets, conserving the earth's resources, and supporting reliable relief agencies with skill as well as money.

Many years ago on one of his trips to the interior of China, Bob Pierce visited a mission school-orphanage run by German sisters near the Tibetan border. While viewing the facilities, his attention was drawn to a forlorn little creature, her razor-thin body hunched at the bottom of the old stone steps. No more than 10, her thin face and sad eyes reflected years of hardship and pain.

When Pierce asked why she wasn't admitted, the sister replied, "We have no room."

Pierce was aghast at her reply. "Surely one child won't make that much difference," he reasoned. "Couldn't you make room for just one more?"

The sister sadly answered, "We've made room for 'just one more' time and time again. We already have four times the number of children we were originally prepared to care for. I'm feeding three others out of my own rice bowl, as are all the other sisters. If we don't draw the line somewhere, there'll not be enough rice to keep alive the children we already have."

Pierce persisted, "That's ridiculous. A child comes asking for help and is turned away at the door. Why isn't something being done?"

At this point the sister swept the little girl off the ground and thrust her into Pierce's arms. "What are you going to do about it?"

For a brief moment Pierce was taken aback by her forthright question. He could dig in his pocket and give the sister the money it would take to support that little girl till he could send more. That's exactly what he did.

Incidentally, our compassion can be made doubly compassionate if we do our kindnesses with humility so as not to embarrass the recipient. Some well-to-do believers in India used to quietly leave food on the doorsteps of the poor in the middle of the night. Jesus referred to this type of giving when He said, "But when thou doest alms, let not thy left hand know what thy right hand doeth, that thine alms may be in secret; and thy Father which seeth in secret Himself shall reward thee openly" (Matt. 6:3-4).

His Compassion on the Sick

In contrast to the hardheartedness of the Pharisees who didn't care about a man with a withered hand, Jesus was moved with compassion on the multitude when He saw their sick, so that He healed them (Mark 3:5; Matt. 14:14).

Charles Slattery estimates that "of Christ's recorded miracles, 21 were for the relief of the sick in mind or body. That three-fifths of His recorded miracles had to do with physical suffering is eloquent testimony of His sympathy with the pain, lassitude, or limitation of our common sicknesses."

Pointing out that Jesus never used His power for His own comfort, safety, or benefit, Slattery continues, "If one were to select one trait which the miracles chiefly set forth in Christ's character, that trait would be compassion. Compassion for others made Him exert this superhuman power at times when its exercise was for Himself most dangerous." Acts of healing brought such fame that wild talk of making Him king precipitated the crisis which ended in crucifixion (Charles Slattery, *The Master of the World,* Longmans, Green, and Company, pp. 185-186).

Jesus' compassion is specifically mentioned in connection with certain maladies.

Compassion on the blind. One day two blind men, one named Bartimaeus, sitting by the highway begging, and hearing that Jesus was passing by, persisted in their pleas for mercy. Matthew records, "So Jesus had compassion on them, and touched their eyes, and immediately their eyes received sight, and they followed Him" (20:30-34).

Blindness was widespread in ancient times, aggravated by the glare of sun and sand. The blind were pathetic sights, clad in rags, begging for morsels from passersby. Up to a century ago, 95 percent of the world's blind were paupers, beggars, or confined to institutions. Though philanthrophy and Braille have diminished the pain of the blind, blindness is still a terrible affliction. Who hasn't been moved by the sight of a person with dark glasses, a tin cup, and tapping cane? One blind man told how he hated to go to sleep, for he would wake up thinking it was still dark. He would also dream he could see but woke to a nightmare because he couldn't.

Latest statistics from the World Health Organization report 42 million blind persons in the world, with over 6 million in the United States. Blindness increases in the U.S. by around 35,000 annually. Jesus commanded us to give special consideration to "the poor, the maimed, the lame, the blind" (Luke 14:13).

Compassion on lepers. Leprosy is found in almost every country in the world. Since many nations make no effort to register lepers, the exact total is unknown, though between 12-15 million people are believed to have it today, with about 2,500 in the United States. Today a drug which costs only $1 a year can arrest the disease, but it must be carefully administered.

Society has been cruel to lepers, burning them alive, starving them. As recently as 1957, 10 lepers were killed and 21 injured near Pusan, Korea, in a fracas that broke out because lepers were too near the city.

In the Middle Ages some countries required lepers to wear gray garments, to carry a bell to ring to warn approaching persons of a leper's presence, to step off the road when someone passed by, and to never wash in the river. A church in Canterbury, England, had a little opening in one wall, called a leper's squint; lepers were not permitted in the church but could look through this opening.

In Jesus' day leprosy isolated the victim from family, friends, job, and synagogue. He survived by begging crusts of bread. His mouth was to be always covered, except when crying out "Unclean!" The leper was considered hopeless, even dead.

One day a leper suddenly loomed in front of Jesus, a hideous, disfigured sight for he was "full of leprosy" (Luke 5:12). In desperation he begged for healing. Moved with compassion, Jesus touched him, saying, "Be thou clean" (v. 13). The leper was immediately and completely healed. Jesus could have shouted, "Be healed, but don't get close to Me." Instead, He gave the leper an uplift by touching an untouchable.

Compassion on a demon-possessed man. Among the most striking stories in the Gospels is the healing of the Gadarene demoniac whose strength was so fierce that he could break any chain binding him. He roamed the mountains, yelling and cutting himself with sharp stones. Healed by Jesus and found sitting, clothed and in his right mind, the ex-demoniac understandably wanted to stay in Jesus' company. But Jesus told him to go back to his friends and tell them how the Lord had done great things for him and "hath had compassion on thee" (Mark 5:19).

Though the previously mentioned healings were specifically the results of Jesus' compassion, certainly all His other cures sprang from compassion too. Compassion should be the trademark of Jesus' followers. Jesus held up as a worthy example the Good Samaritan who "had compassion on" the wounded victim (Luke 10:33).

My wife and I are the parents of seven lovely daughters. But when our eighth girl was born a mongoloid, though she lived less than an hour it opened up a new world to us. It influenced me to write an article on Uncle Win's *Camp Hope* 55 miles north of New York City, where he handles hundreds of mentally retarded children every summer and has an all-year-round permanent home as well. My wife took college courses in special education and became a substitute teacher under the public school system for trainable and educable children.

Telling how her neighbor was converted, a lady said it began when their fourth child was born brain-damaged. "It was a very difficult time. We didn't know that across the street was a couple who also had a brain-damaged child. These neighbors began to observe how people in our church came over to help and support us. They saw something that was very real and out of the ordinary. As a result our neighbors were born again and became active members of our church, touched by the genuine compassion they witnessed."

His Compassion on the Sorrowing

Three instances of Christ raising the dead are recorded in the Gospels: the 12-year-old daughter of Jairus, the son of the widow of Nain, and Lazarus. None of these was raised primarily for his own benefit, for all were far better off in that fairer land. Even though they were revived, they would still pass away later. But Jesus raised them because of His compassion on their surviving loved ones.

Observing the funeral procession of a young man, the only son of his widowed mother, Jesus "had compassion on her, and said unto her, 'Weep not.' Then touching the coffin, He said, 'Young man, I say unto thee, Arise.' And he that was dead sat up and began to speak. And He delivered him to his mother" (Luke 7:12-15).

Have you ever watched mourners in a funeral procession? I've witnessed such scenes in Portugal, Italy, and even in a remote island in the China Sea. Shuffling along, bereft women lean heavily on the arms of loved ones, handkerchiefs dabbing at wet eyes which stare glassily.

That day Jesus saw a mother weeping over the loss of her son. Without any request to do anything, without sermonizing or philosophizing on the glories of the world to come, yet moved by compassion, He restored the boy to his grieving mother.

Two elements seemed to have intensified Jesus' compassion: she was a widow, and the boy was her only son. Incidentally, Jairus' daughter was an only child (Luke 8:42); Lazarus, apparently an only brother.

A young father who had just experienced the painful loss of his wife in death took his little girl home after the funeral. Alone in the house for the first time since the mother's passing, they retired for the night. After a period with the lights out, the child softly asked, "Daddy, are you there?"

He answered that he was close by. Then a moment later, "Daddy is your face turned this way?"

Assured that his face was turned toward her, she went to sleep.

No matter the sorrow, the child of God can know that the eye of Christ is fixed toward us with all His care and compassion.

His Compassion on the Shepherdless

Jesus certainly had compassion on the multitudes. He fed them. He healed them. He sometimes raised their dead. But supremely He saw them as sheep having no shepherd, fainting and scattered abroad (Matt. 9:36).

Likening us to sheep is not a complimentary analogy. Sheep are silly and stupid. They so easily go astray, following the animal in front of them. They are helpless and dirty, never cleansing themselves like cats do. They spend half their lives bleating because of the thorns or burrs caught in their fleeces. Lost humanity is so sheeplike. But the Good Shepherd loves us. The parable of the lost sheep reflects the compassion of the seeking Saviour who came into the world to seek and save wandering sheep.

At a poolside barbecue a man suddenly ran across the patio and jumped into the water. He surfaced a minute later, holding a small limp body in his arms. The police were called, but the little girl could not be revived. Her father had left her mother, who was now thinking of marrying a man who would only go through with the marriage if her mother would get rid of her. Her mother had actually walked downtown on the streets asking strangers, "Do you want a little girl?"

Accidentally falling into the pool one day, the little girl learned she could get attention that way. In the next two months she nearly drowned four times, but someone always jumped in to save her. But that day with 20 adults making a big noise around the pool, her leap had gone unnoticed for a while.

Many are like her. Desperate for love, they submerge themselves, not in a pool, but in drugs, sex, rock music, or whatever. The plan works for a while, but ultimately the supposed solution becomes the thing that drowns them. The swimming pool didn't provide love and understanding for the little girl. It was whoever jumped in to rescue her. Central truth of the Gospel is that, because of His great compassion for us, Jesus Christ jumped into the world to save us. He won't ignore any who call on Him for help. He's like the father in the parable of the prodigal son, who seeing his boy a great way off, "had compassion, and ran, and fell on his neck, and kissed him" (Luke 15:20).

The compassionate Shepherd wants us to have this same compassion toward lost sheep. T. J. Bach, General Director of TEAM from 1928-46, was converted while a student in Copenhagen, Denmark. Walking down a street on a Sunday afternoon, he noticed a young man crossing the street to give him a tract. Bach crushed the tract in his hand, muttering that people should mind their own business. The young man did not respond but instead turned into a doorway to pray, as tears began to run down his cheeks. Thought Bach, "He has given his money to buy the tract. He has given his time to distribute it. And now he has given his heart in prayer for me."

The young man's compassion toward Bach's crude behavior brought deep conviction. Half an hour later in his room Bach pasted the tract together. He was down on his knees, asking God for forgiveness before he finished reading it. That evening he went to a gospel hall and gave his testimony of how he had found Christ that very day.

Not only does the Lord Jesus want the shepherdless won to Himself, but He also wants them taught. Seeing many people, the Lord "was moved with compassion toward them . . . and He began to teach them many things" (Mark 6:34). Compassion will help us obey the Great Commission which involves both evangelizing and discipling the lost.

A summary document of the Consultation on World Evangelization in Thailand in the summer of 1980 said, "Of all the tragic needs of human beings none is greater than their alienation from their Creator and the terrible reality of eternal death for those who refuse to repent and believe. If therefore we do not commit ourselves with urgency to the task of evangelization, we are guilty of an inexcusable lack of human compassion."

How to Get Compassion

First, compassion comes when we realize how much we have been the recipients of God's compassion. Comprehending the enormity of the debt Christ has forgiven us, we should discover compassion stirring in our hearts for others.

Second, by use of our imagination compassion can be stimulated. Abraham Lincoln once said, "I am sorry for the man who can't feel the whip when it is layed on another man's back." Compassion means "to feel with." Let the healthy wonder what life is like for those confined to the four walls of a hospital. Let the mature imagine how it feels to be young with the youth's fears, temptations, and misgivings. Let the youth picture what it means to be old and unable to move with agility. Let the well-to-do wonder what poverty must be like. And let those with ample brain power put themselves in the shoes of a mentally retarded person.

Thirdly, experience sometimes teaches us compassion. God told Israel to be kind to strangers for they themselves were once strangers in Egypt. Suffering should mellow us and mold us into ministers of compassion. Those who have lost a child can sympathize when someone else loses a child.

Charles Colson who spent time in prison has enormous sympathy for those in jail. Founder of *Prison Fellowship,* he leads a ministry that reaches into over 100 American prisons. In 1979, 70 week-long

"In-Prison Seminars" were held in 40 states and 30 federal institutions. Over 250 inmates have graduated from their Washington Seminar program which involves furloughed federal inmates spending two weeks of intensive Bible study and discipleship training in the nation's capital. The writer of Hebrews thanked his readers because they "had compassion on the prisoners" (10:34, RSV).

Years ago a retired nurse visited the baby ward of a large hospital where she had been supervisor a decade before. Looking at the charts, she was puzzled by an entry she had never seen "TLC—three times daily." When she saw a nurse pick up a baby and fondle it, she thought, *How unprofessional.* Then she wondered again about the new drug, TLC. When no one was looking she looked through the prescription file, but TLC was not mentioned. Swallowing her pride, she cornered a young intern, "Doctor, what's this new medicine, TLC? I've seen it on so many charts."

Grinning, the intern pointed to a baby, gurgling happily. "Two months ago, this infant was skin and bones, not expected to live. Medicines didn't help. His recovery was due to TLC."

"You mean TLC is not a medicine?" the surprised nurse asked.

"Not from a bottle, yet it's the greatest medicine ever discovered. Some babies die without it. TLC stands for Tender Loving Care."

Despite the sterilized bottle, restricted contact, and glass-enclosed nurseries, the mortality rate was lowered only when tender loving care was present.

A man, browsing among the weather-beaten tombstones of a century-old English graveyard, came across an inscription which had been kept clean and legible. It said merely, "He was compassionate." Whoever this long-expired stranger was—he had the kind of heart Christ possessed and wants us to have.

5
The Prayerfulness of Jesus

To many people in our scientific, materialistic age, prayer seems unnecessary and unrelated to day by day living. Many would say with the philosopher Santanyana, "Prayer is painting your wishes against the clouds. When they come true, you call it answered prayer. When they don't, you call it submission to the Almighty."

Some who have succumbed to naturalism and discarded the reality of prayer could sadly say with Thomas Hood,

>I remember, I remember
>The fir trees dark and high;
>I used to think their slender tops
>Were close against the sky;
>It was a childish ignorance,
>But now 'tis little joy
>To know I'm further off from heav'n
>Than when I was a boy.

Supernaturalists set forth many arguments for the possibility of answered prayer. But the most clinching argument for the power of prayer is the simple fact that Jesus prayed. If the Son of God, Creator, and Sustainer of the universe, found it necessary to cry out for help and wisdom, how much more we frail, faltering humans need to pray.

Prayer Dominated His Life

Prayer was the habit of Jesus' life. Over 20 times His praying is mentioned in the four Gospels, over half in Luke which emphasizes His humanity. At every major crisis He prayed: baptism, selection of disciples, transfiguration, Gethsemane, Calvary. Since prayer played such a great part in His life, it ought to in ours as well. Let's look at several characteristics of Jesus' praying.

Regular. Jesus' prayer life was regular. As a devout member of the Jewish populace, He probably faithfully observed the custom of praying three times daily, morning, afternoon at the time of daily sacrifice, and sunset when the temple gates were shut. The early disciples continued this practice (Acts 3:1; 10: 3, 9, 30).

Mark records, "In the morning, rising up a great while before day, He went out, and departed into a solitary place, and there prayed (1:35). After the feeding of the 5,000 He was alone at the close of the day on a mountain where He had gone to pray (Matt. 14:23). When surrounded by the crowd, clamoring for His attention, He "withdrew Himself into the wilderness, and prayed" (Luke 5:16). Probably, this was a scheduled time for prayer, a spiritual exercise He engaged in before He faced His duties every day.

Not only did He have regular times for prayer, but favorite places as well, like the desert or the Mount of Olives. Luke wrote, "He came out, and went, as he was wont, to the Mount of Olives" (22:39).

Impressive. Jesus prayed not only alone, but often in the presence of others. He blessed the loaves and fish with 5,000 present. He prayed midst a sorrowing group before raising Lazarus. He asked the help of His heavenly Father publicly when Greeks came to see Him. His prayers from the cross were audible to the mob.

Jesus prayed many times in the hearing of His disciples, practicing a sort of family altar (Luke 9:18). They noted the priority of prayer in their Master's life. They also became painfully aware of their own deficiency—His praying was so impressive. Once, after hearing His beautiful prayer, as soon as He sounded His "Amen," one of the Twelve blurted out, "Lord, teach us to pray, as John also taught his disciples" (Luke 11:1). They seemed ashamed to continue formulating their requests with such stumbling, inadequate words.

The model prayer that followed, commonly known as the Lord's Prayer, has been called the alphabet of all petition. Major elements of spiritual desire are summed up in a few choice requests. Of the six requests, the first three refer to God's glory, the other three to man's good. This model was not meant to bind us to a stereotyped approach to God, but to provide direction in the expression and development of our prayer life.

Persistent. Right after giving the model prayer, Jesus taught persistence in prayer. To illustrate this truth, He told the parable of the troubled friends who begged for three loaves of bread at midnight to set before an unexpected guest. Jesus concluded, "Ask, and it shall be given you; seek, and ye shall find: knock, and it shall be opened unto you (vv. 5-10).

Jesus taught, "Men ought always to pray, and not to faint" (18:1). Then He reinforced His teaching with the story of the unfair judge who finally granted a mistreated widow her request, not because of justice, but because her continual coming wore Him down.

Jesus never said, "Understand prayer," but "Pray." All rational arguments against prayer fade in the light of Jesus' example, teachings, and commands. His whole life breathed the atmosphere of prayer. Significantly, Jesus never taught His disciples how to preach, but He did teach them how to pray.

What Jesus Prayed For

Though the items for which Jesus prayed may be classified in many ways, we categorize them under three areas: consecration, dependence, and intercession. (Chapter 6 deals with His prayers of gratitude.)

Consecration. Jesus dedicated new ventures to His heavenly Father. For example, at the very outset of His public ministry, He prayed. "Now when all the people were baptized, it came to pass, that Jesus also being baptized, and praying, the heaven was opened" (Luke 3:21). The grammar suggests a continuing activity in prayer, interrupted by the booming, approving voice from heaven.

Why was Jesus baptized? Not to symbolize the forgiveness of sins, for He had none to forgive. But to identify with us, the sinners. Since He would ultimately die for us, He identified with us at the beginning of His mission.

His baptism marked His embarkation on His public ministry. As He stood on this inaugural day, about to go forth to bear the load of the world's iniquities, He may well have prayed, "Lo, I come to do Thy will, O God" (Heb. 10:9). Standing on the threshold of His itinerant campaigning, perhaps He prayed, "My teaching, My miracles, My healings, My death, I dedicate to Thee. See Me through. May I finish My course now set before Me with joy."

An excellent time to pray is at the start of a new chapter. Not when we have tried and failed, though prayer may be essential then. Not as a last resort, but in the fresh dawn at life's beginnings we should pray for divine blessing.

Just before Jesus first revealed to His disciples the alarming prospect of His approaching death, "He was alone praying" (Luke 9:18). Godet's commentary suggests that Jesus, anticipating the startling impression such news would make on His disciples, prepared Himself in prayer.

Many folks have gone to their knees on New Year's Eve, dedicating to Christ the next 12 months with all its uncertainity. Some families at the start of an automobile trip, bow their heads in the car, and ask divine protection. Ground breaking for a new building, a visitation campaign, an evangelistic crusade, the commissioning of a missionary—all these are fitting occasions for the prayer of consecration.

Prayer is especially appropriate at the start of every day. Earlier we noted our Lord's praying very early in the morning. An example of a busy day in Jesus' life, as noted by A.T. Robertson, is found in the Gospel of Mark. In the forenoon Jesus taught a large crowd, some of whom insulted Him, while others demanded a sign. After a while, His mother and brother tried to spirit Him away, thinking Him unstable. In the afternoon He told a group of parables, several of which He interpreted privately. Toward night He crossed the Sea of Galilee in a boat, so tired He fell asleep during a storm severe enough for the fearful disciples to wake Him up. Then He healed the Gadarene demoniac and returned by boat, apparently the same evening. Robertson suggests that this was just one of many similar days in the Master's ministry (*Harmony of the Gospels,* Harper and Row, p. 61). No wonder Jesus went out early in the morning to pray (Mark 1:35).

In that hectic final week of Jesus' life He taught in the temple to the early-morning crowd. But nights He spent on the Mount of Olives praying, both on retiring and on early rising for the tasks of the new day (Luke 21:37-38).

Dependence. No more important issue, except the cross, would Jesus face than the selection of His disciples. Who would be the chosen ones to successfully guide Christianity through those early decades of persecution, misunderstanding, and problems?

The men to whom Jesus entrusted the establishment of His church would have to be willing to learn and to die for His cause. He couldn't choose millionaires, scholars, or socialites, for likely they wouldn't be sufficiently poor in spirit. Wisdom was needed.

No wonder Jesus climbed a mountain and spent all night in a prayer vigil before making the choices. "He went out into a mountain to pray, and continued all night in prayer to God. And when it was day, He called unto Him His disciples; and of them He chose 12 whom also He named apostles" (Luke 6:12-13).

Then follow the names of the Twelve. What an unlikely crew! The disciples, if they had a say, probably never would have chosen each other. Peter was unstable, Andrew colorless, John and James hotheads, Thomas a doubter, Simon a fanatic for his own nation, and Matthew a seeming traitor since he sold his services as a tax collector to Rome.

In utter dependence on His heavenly Father, Jesus made the selection. The rest is history: these men, even though one defected, changed the course of history and the face of the globe.

Before performing miracles the Lord often prayed in reliance on His Father. When healing a deaf man who also had a speech impediment, Jesus took the victim aside. Touching his ears and tongue then looking up to heaven, doubtless in prayer, He said, "Be opened." Immediately the man heard and spoke plainly (Mark 7:31-37).

Jesus depended on His Father for power. When the disciples

could not exorcise a demon from a possessed boy, Jesus gave this reason, "This kind can come forth by nothing, but by prayer and fasting" (Mark 9:29).

During His final week the Lord Jesus received a visit from certain Greeks. Though mystery surrounds their exact purpose, some Bible teachers believe their coming was a major temptation. Perhaps they were inviting Him to become their teacher, luring Him to an appealing occupation which would sidetrack Him from the cross. Thus His statement, "Except a corn of wheat fall into the ground and die, it abideth alone; but if it die, it bringeth forth much fruit. . . . Now is My soul troubled, and what shall I say? Father, save Me from this hour: but for this cause came I unto this hour. Father, glorify Thy name" (John 12:24, 27-28). Jesus' cry of dependence did not go unheeded, whatever His need may have been. "Then came there a voice from heaven, saying 'I have both glorified it, and will glorify it, and will glorify it again'" (John 12:28).

Incidentally, all three times the Father's voice came from heaven were occasions when Jesus had prayed: at His baptism, at His transfiguration, and at this crisis.

A supreme example of Jesus' prayer of dependence was His pleading in Gethsemane. It was the night before the great sacrifice. Satan would be crushed as the Saviour became sin for us. Nowhere was our Lord's manhood more evident than when He shrank away from the thought of His own death, which was typified by the drinking of the cup. In agony He offered up "prayers and supplications with strong crying and tears" (Heb. 5:7). Then with renewed strength He could face the ordeal of arrest, trial, and the cross.

Prayer was our Lord's way of showing His utter reliance on His Father. All He did and spoke came from the power and wisdom of Him who sent Him. Prayer affirmed His soul's active alignment with the Father's will. Even in His exclamation of abandonment on the cross, "My God, My God, why has Thou forsaken Me?" He was groping for renewed fellowship with His Father (Matt. 27:46). Certainly, His final word from the cross was one of reliance, "Father, into Thy hands I commend My spirit" (Luke 23:46).

As burdens pressed in on the Lord Jesus, so they will on us. When they do, we should tread His steps by throwing our reliance on our Father in heaven.

A friend said to the founder of a thriving missionary society, "It must give you deep satisfaction to be chosen by God to start this vast enterprise." The founder replied, "It seemed to me that God looked over the whole world to find a man who was weak enough to do His work, and when He at last found me, He said, 'He is weak enough—he'll do!'"

We need to make this declaration of dependence, "Lord, without You we can do nothing."

Intercession. Jesus prayed for others. The most vivid instance of His intercessory prayer involved Peter. Knowing that Peter would deny Him, Jesus promised, "Simon, Simon, behold, Satan hath desired to have you, that he may sift you as wheat. But I have prayed for thee, that thy faith fail not; and when thou art converted, strengthen thy brethren" (Luke 22:31-32).

Jesus knew Peter's weakness, and told him that He had already interceded in His behalf. Despite Peter's protests of loyalty, within hours the boastful apostle had denied Christ three times. When reminded of his defection by the crowing of the cock, he went out and wept bitterly. Until restored by the Lord in a private meeting on the resurrection morn, Peter must have died a thousand deaths as remorse tore at his heart because of his gross infidelity. Why didn't Peter go out and hang himself? A partial answer might be—Jesus' intercession. Incidentally, the only time Jesus spoke of His private prayer life was when He mentioned His prayer for Peter.

A former teacher of mine at Moody Bible Institute told how when serving as a missionary in Korea, he awoke one night concerned for George, a Korean convert. His wife tried to quiet him, "You're overwrought and nervous."

The missionary insisted George was in trouble. "I must get up and pray for him."

Later George told about that night—how he had been captured and tortured. But he said, "Then Jesus came, and it was all right." The missionary knew then that his intercessory prayer had been divinely directed and honored.

What an example of intercession is Jesus' high-priestly prayer recorded in John 17. By all logic the disciples should have been comforting Jesus who was about to suffer the unimaginable ordeal of the cross. Instead, He comforted them, and prayed for them. Because this flock would soon be left defenseless in a world of ravenous wolves, Jesus committed them to His Father's Care.

Knowing that envy and strife could puncture the disciples' spiritual kinship, Jesus prayed "That they may be one" (v. 11).

Satan, the enemy of souls, would try to destroy the disciples. With this in mind, Jesus prayed that the Father would: keep them from the evil one" (v. 15, NEB).

Sensing their deep sorrow because of His coming departure, Jesus prayed for reunion with them beyond the grave. Father, I desire "that they also . . . be with me where I am; that they may behold My glory, which Thou hast given Me" (v. 24).

How gratifying to know that also in that prayer He remembered all believers who would follow through the centuries. If you are a believer, He prayed that night for your security, sanctification, and ultimate safe lodging with Him in glory (vv. 20-26). He told His Father, "Neither pray I for these alone, but for them also which shall believe on Me through their word."

Even on the cross the Lord interceded for others. As they cruelly pounded nails through His hands and feet, stabbing Him with excruciating pain, His first cry midst anguish and torment was, "Father, forgive them; for they know not what they do" (Luke 23:34). His prayer was answered, for so outrageous was their crime of crucifying the Son of God that, had He not prayed, judgment might have struck, dispatching every participant in the crime into eternal damnation. But intercession held back the storm. Also, in a few minutes a thief at His side repented. The centurion was deeply moved, "Truly this was the Son of God" (Matt. 27:54). At Pentecost 3,000 believed, undoubtedly many of those who had shouted "Crucify Him!" A few months later a great company of the priests came to believe on Him (Acts 6:7).

During an early year meeting at Montrose Bible Conference, a Bible teacher from Australia, Dr. L. Sale-Harrison, spoke to Dr. R. A. Torrey, founder of the conference. He asked, "Do you realize that the outstanding Christian laymen of Australia today are men converted in your revival campaigns there 27 years ago?'

Dr. Torrey's face lit up, "Can you give me any of their names?"

After thinking a minute, Dr. Sale-Harrison proceeded to name half a dozen. As the names were mentioned, Dr. Torrey's eyes grew moist. "During those campaigns I asked the Christian workers for a list of the young men converted who seemed to have promising futures as believers. I have had that list for 27 years, and have prayed daily since that time for these young men. I recognize some of the names you mention."

Family members can have an important ministry by praying for each other. At the start of every year one set of parents mails a dozen postcards to each of their children, promising that if each month they mail a card with their urgent prayer requests, these needs will be taken before the throne of grace in parental intercessory prayer. One mother calls her grown children periodically to ask for their prayer requests. They, in turn, ask hers, and each remembers the other in prayer.

Sometimes when we have so many requests to remember, we don't know where to start. Dr. Stephen Olford, well-known evangelist, suggests the following daily breakdown of requests: on Monday, missionaries; Tuesday, tasks; Wednesday, workers; Thursday, thanks; Friday, family; Saturday, saints; Sunday, sinners.

Though the record gives no indication that the disciples profited from Jesus' caring prayers before He went to the cross, after the ascension it was a different story. They had been transformed. They met for prayer in the Upper Room before Pentecost. Then in those early days of the church they continued steadfastly in prayer (Acts 2:42). Prayer *does* make a difference. We can be changed just as the disciples were—by the power of prayer.

6
The Thankfulness of Jesus

Eleanor MacKerron, well-known evangelistic pianist, and organist for many years at New Hampshire's Rumney Bible Conference, underwent a brain operation due to meningitis in the mid 1960s. Surgeons removed the decompression bone from her skull.

Seven years later a lady came up to her at Rumney Bible Conference with the startling news, "I have your skull bone." Introducing herself as a nurse at New London Submarine Hospital in Connecticut, she told how a few years before she had been hit on the head by a beam at the submarine base. Facing a brain operation at New England Baptist Hospital, she needed a bone. Doctors found the exact size from their bone bank. She asked to whom it had belonged. The answer, "Eleanor MacKerron." She said to herself, "Some day I'll find her and thank her." As the nurse thanked her, Eleanor MacKerron reached out and felt her bone in someone else's head.

An abounding spirit of gratitude should saturate the inner life of every Christian. Because the Lord "daily loadeth us with benefits" (Ps. 68:19) we should say with the psalmist, "Every day I will bless Thee" (145:2). Daniel gave thanks three times daily (Dan. 6:10). We are told to "offer the sacrifice of praise . . . continually" (Heb. 13:15). Paul makes much of thankfulness in his epistles. Six times in Colossians he mentions it (1:3, 12; 2:7; 3:15, 17; 4:2). A thankful spirit is evidence of a Spirit-filled life (Eph. 5:18-20).

Jesus Christ, who possessed the Spirit without measure owned a thankful spirit. Besides the unconscious ways in which His appreciation comes through for many common blessings in life, like birds, flowers, grass, fish, sheep, vines, and little children, He expressed specific gratitude on several occasions. If the Lord of glory bothered to say thanks, how much more should feeble, finite humans possess an attitude of appreciation. We should be thankful, not only *for* Him, but *like* Him.

He Was Thankful for Food

All four Gospels record Jesus' thanks before meals. Before the feeding of the 5,000 He "took the five loaves, and the two fishes, and looking up to heaven, He blessed, and brake, and gave the loaves to His disciples, and the disciples to the multitude" (Matt. 14:19).

Some Christians today are ashamed to bow their heads in a restaurant or small social gathering and silently thank God for their food. Yet the Lord bowed His head before more than 5,000 people and audibly voiced His gratitude. He followed the same procedure at the feeding of the 4,000. In fact, at this miracle he gave thanks twice, both for the bread and for the fish (Mark 8:6-7).

Giving thanks for bread and fish encompasses a vast area of divine power. Tracing the history of the loaves takes us back to the fields where the grain grew and to the skies from which the showers dropped. Similarly, the fish lead us back to stream, river, and lake. Giving of thanks before meals in the Saviour's spirit envelops a wide sweep of outlook including bounties of sky, sea, and earth.

According to Paul, meats have been created by God and are "to be received with thanksgiving of them which believe and know the truth. For every creature of God is good, and nothing to be refused, if it be received with thanksgiving: for it is sanctified by the Word of God and prayer" (1 Tim. 4:3-5).

On a visit to Haiti in 1980 to observe the ministries of World Relief Corporation, I shall never forget seeing 300 boys and girls each served a hot bowl of food at noon recess in a school a few miles outside Port au Prince. This was part of a quarter million dollar program which feeds 15,000 children a meal five days a week. For some this is the only meal they get each day. Nor shall I ever forget the song of grace they sang before they ate, "Merci, merci, merci" ("Thanks, thanks, thanks").

Yet in our greatly blessed America, the once-prevalent practice of saying grace is fast fading from the scene. One Christian whose duties took him coast to coast remarked that he had eaten in restaurants from New York to Los Angeles and had not seen more than five people bow their heads in public, even to silently say grace.

Perhaps a trip abroad would soon enlighten Americans to their God-blessed, bountiful supply of food. In a poor hill tribe in Columbia, South America, a Christian national could not understand the meaning of the New Testament word *gluttonous*. Even after explanation that a glutton is one who eats excessively, he could scarcely grasp its significance, simply because he rarely ever had enough to satisfy his hunger.

A few years ago when Nikita Khrushchev visited the States, we did not let him hear us call on God to bless the food. When he was entertained at dinner at the White House, no blessing was asked. Officials of New York City dispensed with the blessing at a civic function at the Commodore Hotel. Business leaders at the Economic Club dinner did not thank God for the food. Brought over here to see how we live, Khrushchev could rightly have concluded that saying grace is a disappearing custom.

But some people still have the courage of their convictions. A Christian farmer visiting the city for a day entered a restaurant for his noon meal. When the food was served he quietly bowed his head and gave silent thanks. A young man at the next table, trying to embarrass him, called out in a loud voice, "Hey, farmer, does everyone do that out in the country where you live?" The farmer calmly replied, "No, son, the pigs don't."

The disciples could never forget that Jesus said grace before feeding the 5,000. About 60 years later, John, in identifying a certain place in Jesus' travels, referred to the miracle. "Howbeit there came other boats from Tiberias nigh unto the place where they did eat bread, after that the Lord had given thanks" (John 6:23). The offering of thanks loomed as memorable as the miracle of the loaves and fishes. Gratitude for food should be important to us, just as it was to Jesus.

He Was Thankful for Spiritual Insight Given to the Simple

Jesus gave thanks because His heavenly Father had revealed spiritual truth to the ignorant and had hidden such matters from the clever. "I thank Thee, O Father, Lord of heaven and earth, because Thou hast hid these things from the wise and prudent, and hast revealed them unto babes" (Matt. 11:25).

The Lord did not mean that intellectual attainment automatically blocked faith, but that it was unnecessary for true belief. The most untutored person can apprehend saving truth concerning Christ. Lack of learning does not disqualify. On the other hand, ignorance may have its advantage. Those who humbly realize their emptiness are more readily receptive to divine wisdom than those smugly filled with their own learning. Know-it-alls have little room for more knowledge.

Jesus continually hid things from wise skeptics and learned unbelievers but revealed truth to His simple, unpretentious disciples. The Pharisess asked for a sign, but He gave them none except that of the Prophet Jonah (12:38ff). When His disciples asked for a sign, His answer covered the space of two chapters (chaps. 24—25).

One reason Jesus spoke in parables was to continue the confusion of disbelievers. He told His disciples, "Because it is given unto you to know the mysteries of the kingdom of heaven, but to them it is not given. . . . Therefore speak I to them in parables; because they seeing see not; and hearing they hear not, neither do they understand" (13:10-13). Then He proceeded to explain to the disciples privately the meaning of the parables He had uttered publicly.

The proud Pharisees did not believe His deity, but this basic truth was revealed to simple Peter (Matt. 16:16-18). When Jesus healed a man born blind, the Pharisees would not accept this miracle, despite the evidence. He commented, "For judgment I am come into this world, that they which see not might see; and that they which see might be made blind" (John 9:39). The blind man saw both physically and spiritually. But the Pharisees, who claimed to have the light, were shown to be really blind.

Those who did not wish to know the truth received no light from the Lord. When Jesus was sent from Pilate to Herod to be judged, the latter hoped Jesus would perform some miracle. But Jesus did no miracle just to satisfy the whim of a wicked unbeliever to merely see "magic" (Luke 23:8). At Jesus' trial, the high priest insincerely asked Him about His teaching. Jesus in effect replied, "I spoke openly to the world. Why ask me? Ask those who heard Me." (cf. John 18:20-21). The questioners marveled at His silence.

Jesus seemed to confuse the so-called wise but confirmed the faith of humble believers. After the resurrection He did not appear to unbelieving enemies like Pilate, Annas, Caiaphas, the Roman soldiers, the Herodians, the Sadducees, or the Pharisees. He knew they would be unconvinced even by His personal appearance. But He did show Himself to His followers.

Paul described the members of the early church as, "Not many wise men after the flesh, not many mighty, not many noble" (1 Cor. 1:26). Not many of the intellectuals like Gamaliel, not many of the influential like Felix or Festus, not many of the illustrious like Agrippa or Nero were found in evangelical ranks. Rather they were ordinary people, often without education, described by second century historian Celsus as "wool-workers, cobblers, leather-dressers and the most clownish of men," who constituted the major segment of the church.

But it doesn't say not *any* wise men. Through the centuries some of the nobles like Pascal, Bacon, Wilberforce, Disraeli, have believed. But they have always been a minority. As a rule, spiritual truth has been revealed to the unimportant and hidden from VIPs.

It's possible to know all about rocks but not to know the Rock of Ages; to know all about flowers but not to be acquainted with the Rose of Sharon and the Lily of the Valley; to understand much about light but not to follow the Light of the world. Jesus was thankful because you don't have to be in *Who's Who* to know what's what.

He Was Thankful for Answered Prayer

The humanity and deity of Jesus blended beautifully at the grave of Lazarus. In sorrow Jesus wept at the loss of a beloved friend. While tears were trickling down those holy cheeks, He cried with the voice of power, "Lazarus, come forth!" Between those demonstrations of manhood and Godhood, Jesus lifted His eyes to heaven and said, "Father, I thank Thee that Thou hast heard Me. And I knew that Thou hearest Me always" (John 11:41-42). Jesus was thankful for a petition-hearing and a prayer-answering Father.

Many psalms are thanksgivings to God for divine answers to prayer. For example, when the Lord rescued David from the hand of King Saul, David broke forth in praise, ending his song, "Therefore will I give thanks unto Thee, O Lord, among the heathen, and sing praises unto Thy name. Great deliverance giveth He to His king" (Ps. 18:49-50). David, who had prayed for rescue, was thankful for answered prayer.

Some months after joining the Air Force a young fellow placed a thousand-mile phone call to his Christian wife's godly aunt. Though not a Christian himself, he begged his aunt-in-law, "Pray for me! Tonight I make my first jump! Even though a bunch of other paratroopers will be jumping, I have to go it alone. I'm number two man, I need prayer! I don't want to worry my wife. I jump around midnight."

The aunt promised. As the clock neared midnight, she slipped to her knees. A thousand miles south a huge bomber taxied across the field and climbed up into the pitch-black sky. No light shone inside or outside. Suddenly a red bulb flashed, the signal for paratrooper number one to jump. Fitfully he turned to number two, "I can't do it!"

Unafraid and calm, the number two man agreed to jump. As he fumbled for the door, he could feel the big bomber tilting. Through the doorway he went.

As his parachute opened, the plane exploded, shooting streaks of fire through the sky. Seconds later the plane crashed in an open field, killing every crew member. Just the lone airman escaped. On furlough he related his experience to members of a Wisconsin church, accepted Christ as his Saviour, and publicly thanked the Lord for answered prayer.

When Paul was delivered from deadly peril through the prayers of caring friends, many thanks were given to the Lord because of his escape (2 Cor. 1:11). Thankfulness for answered prayer reflects the glory of God.

He Was Thankful for His Own Death

Not only was Jesus grateful for food, for spiritual insight given the lowly, and for answered prayer, but He was also thankful for His coming sacrifice at Calvary.

The Gospels state that at the institution of the Lord's Supper, Jesus gave thanks twice, both before breaking the bread and before drinking the wine. These elements symbolized His crucified body and His shed blood. The night before He died, with full knowledge of His imminent sacrifice for sin, He gave thanks for His redemptive death.

In relating how the Lord's Supper was initiated, Paul specifically mentioned the giving of thanks by Jesus before each element (1 Cor. 11:23-25). So vital a part did thanksgiving play in this ordinance that many churches call it the *Eucharist,* which means giving thanks.

That night Jesus knew the significance of the broken bread and of the wine. The moment for which He had been born was upon Him. All the agonies He would experience in those awesome hours were pictured by that bread and wine. Yet He thanked God.

Through Old Testament days lambs and bulls came bleating and bellowing to the brazen altar. But the true Lamb of God opened not His mouth, except to give thanks.

Late one evening the phone rang in a California home. "Mrs. Otto," a voice asked, "did you give a pint of blood to the Red Cross last December 14th?"

Hesitating a moment, Mrs. Otto recalled the occasion. The speaker identified himself as a public relations officer at a nearby military hospital. "I'm sorry to call so late, but a patient has just arrived who wants to meet you."

Mrs. Otto learned that her pint of blood, flown to a battle area in the Orient, had saved this soldier's life. Said the caller, "He wants to thank you, but he leaves early in the morning for the East Coast."

A stunned Mrs. Otto made her way to the hospital. She learned that rarely did a soldier ever meet the person whose blood saved his life. Most blood donations were mixed plasma, but her particular pint of blood had gone into an individual container labeled with the donor's name.

Just before her blood had reached the battle area, the injured sergeant had been fighting for his life. Trapped by the enemy, he was covering the withdrawal of his group when 15 slugs hit him in the left leg. Medical corpsmen carried him to a makeshift field-hospital where his leg was amputated. When he regained consciousness, a doctor handed him the tag from a blood container. "It was this woman's blood which saved your life, Sergeant!"

Clutching the tag, the soldier muttered through clenched teeth, "Maybe some day—I can thank her—for saving my life."

As the sergeant told the story, he wept unashamedly. Mrs. Otto wept too. But how many people have ever wept in thanks for the greatest blood donor of all, the Lord Jesus Christ?

The Lord Jesus notices when people are ungrateful. When only one of ten healed lepers returned to fall prostrate before Him and give thanks, Jesus asked, "But where are the nine?" (Luke 17:17)

Every child of God should have a grateful attitude, not only during the good times of life, but also in the bad times. If Jesus could sing the night before He died (Matt. 26:30), this should be our example. "In everything give thanks: for this is the will of God in Christ Jesus concerning you" (1 Thes. 5:18).

Have you thanked the Lord Jesus Christ for His death in your behalf?

7

The Magnetism of Jesus

On a recent trip to Moncton, New Brunswick, Canada a friend drove me to Magnetic Hill, a tourist attraction 5 miles out of the city. He proceeded to a designated spot, turned off the car's motor, and released the brakes. I then experienced the eerie sensation of rolling uphill. Looking to the side, I saw a stream also flowing uphill. Actually, the experience was an optical illusion, not the result of magnetic forces in the hill.

Then I thought of the real magnetism of Jesus Christ, which displayed itself from the very beginning of His ministry by the constant droves of people who were drawn to Him.

The Crowds

Multitudes, not just individuals, pursued Jesus from His early to ending days. After the call of Peter, Andrew, James and John, Scripture records that the popularity of our Lord's ministry grew so that "there followed Him great multitudes of people from Galilee, and from Decapolis, and from Jerusalem, and from Judaea, and from beyond Jordan" (Matt. 4:18-25).

More than once the press of the crowd was so great that Jesus pushed a borrowed boat out from land to use as a platform from which to teach the people on the shore (Luke 5:1-3; Mark 4:1).

After the healing of Peter's mother-in-law, when the sun was set, the people of Capernaum gathered at the door of Peter's house, bringing all the diseased and demon-possessed, whom Jesus healed (Mark 1:32-34). The next morning His disciples found Him in a desert place and exclaimed, "All men seek for Thee" (v. 37).

Jesus did not play to the grandstand. On the contrary, He repeatedly took special effort to reduce superficial support by requesting those He healed to keep quiet. For instance, after healing a leper He said, "See thou say nothing to any man: but go thy way, show thyself to the priest, and offer for thy cleansing those things which Moses commanded, for a testimony unto them."

But the cured man, delirious in his newfound health, "went out and began to publish it much, and to blaze abroad the matter, insomuch that Jesus could not more openly enter into the city, but was without in desert places: and they came to Him from every quarter" (vv. 44-45). The same broadcasting of Jesus' exploits occurred after He healed the Gadarene demoniac (Luke 8:39).

Back again in Capernaum word noised around that He was likely in Peter's house. Such a crowd congregated that to get a palsied man in for Jesus to heal, his sponsors had to uncover a hole in the roof and lower him at Jesus' feet (Mark 2:1-4).

After choosing His 12 disciples, Jesus descended to a plain where a great multitude had come "to hear Him, and to be healed of their diseases. . . and the whole multitude sought to touch Him" (Luke 6:17-19).

In a crowd a woman with a 12-year history of a blood disease touched the hem of His garment in faith and was healed. Jesus turned about and asked, "Who touched Me?" The disciples reacted, "Thou seest the multitude thronging Thee, and sayest Thou, 'Who touched Me'?" (Mark 5:30-31)

The crowds exceeded 5,000, then 4,000 when He miraculously fed them. In every age the man who can provide food, reduce inflation, and eliminate unemployment can be elected to public office. Jesus knew this as the crowds chased Him around the Sea of Galilee. A little encouragement and they could have made Him king (John 6:15). But Jesus did nothing to seek a temporal throne. Rather His straight-from-the-shoulder remarks resulted in whole-sale defections (v. 66).

Wherever He went He attracted crowds: "a great multitude" (Mark 9:14); "all the people" (John 8:2); "an innumerable multitude of people, insomuch that they trode one upon another" (Luke 12:1); "much people" (John 12:9). Even at the extremity of His country, in a house in the heathen borders of Tyre and Sidon, where He hoped no one would know Him, "He could not be hid" (Mark 7:24).

At the end, the crowd was still there. A multitude accompanied Him through Jericho, and paraded to Bethany to see Lazarus. Jesus rode midst blocks of pilgrims, overflowing the city for Passover. On hearing Jesus was coming to Jerusalem, crowds came to the feast. They greeted Him by waving branches of palm trees and crying, "Hosanna! Blessed is the King of Israel that cometh in the name of the Lord!" (John 12:12-13) At that point the Pharisees conceded, "Behold, the world is gone after Him" (v. 19).

Teaching crowds, preaching to them, feeding, healing, ministering to their needs, Jesus could never be accused of downgrading mass evangelism. His magnetism dramatically drew the multitudes.

Why Did the Crowds Follow Him?

He attracted people because of His caring qualities discussed in this book: His tears, sympathy, gentleness, patience, graciousness, compassion, mercy, love, and forgiving spirit, among others.

Also, He attracted people because of His miracles. And His words likewise astounded them. At the close of the Sermon on the Mount the people were astonished at His doctrine: "For He taught them as one having authority, and not as the scribes" (Matt. 7:28-29).

Jesus did not indulge in flights of rhetoric. His sayings were brief but weighty. His simple style was enhanced by illustrations from everyday life: flowers, soil, birds, sheep. He was a master storyteller. "Without a parable spake He not unto them" (Mark 4:34).

Jesus dealt with vital topics, unlike the Talmud which sometimes branched off into pointless speculation on how God spends time in heaven, or how many angels can dance on the point of a needle, or how a man in the desert can perform his ablutions by using sand.

Jesus summed up the Law as love for God and neighbor, and offered rest for the weary, and pardon for the penitent.

His words were winsome. When rough, burly officers, sent to arrest Him, came back empty-handed, they explained, "Never man spake like this man" (John 7:46).

Character, deeds, and speech all combined to draw people toward Him. How fitting that people who found Him attractive also found Him approachable.

His Approachability

Some people are hard to approach. Getting entree into many of our big-city high-rise apartments is almost impossible. Security officers bar all outsiders unless they can properly identify themselves. Once when I was visiting friends in a large complex in downtown Philadelphia, I was permitted to take the elevator to their eighth floor apartment only because my hosts had previously cleared my name with the information desk.

Some years ago I was assigned to interview the newly crowned world champion heavyweight boxer, Jersey Joe Wolcott. Through the persistence and ingenuity of a photographer-friend, we traced Mr. Wolcott to the Camden, New Jersey area, where we were finally granted an interview with him in a suburban hideout.

But to reach Jesus Christ, no labyrinth of protocol and no red tape can hinder the seeking soul from coming right into His presence. He is easily and immediately accessible.

How hard it is to get an appointment with a doctor. His phone is busy. Or, he's at the hospital on an emergency, and unreachable at the moment. Appointments have to be scheduled weeks beforehand. Then we may have to sit an hour in the waiting room.

But so often the sick got to see the Great Physician immediately. A leper came begging, kneeling, falling on his face. Jesus, available, touched and healed him right there and then (Matt. 8:2-4). In another instance, a woman, who for 12 years had tried every doctor and every cure, touched His robe and was healed immediately (9:20-22).

Multitudes of sick were brought to the door of Peter's house. Though Jesus could have healed en masse by the word of His power,

He "laid His hands on every one of them, and healed them" (Luke 4:40).

Blind Bartimaeus, learning Jesus was near, though discouraged by some of the crowd, persisted till he received an audience with Jesus, and was healed (Mark 10:46-52).

When people came with genuine questions, like the rich young ruler, Jesus never turned them away without an answer. Even when His enemies tried to trip Him up, He was available for an interview.

He was approachable to mothers seeking a blessing for their infants, despite the ill-advised attempt by the disciples to keep them away.

How open He was to the sinner. Though hypocritical religious leaders were scandalized because Jesus associated so freely with outcasts, He indeed was the Friend of publicans and sinners. Zaccheus' desire to see what Jesus looked like probably expressed a subconscious desire for an interview. How typical of Jesus to take the initiative by inviting Himself to the chief tax collector's home.

In His final hours Jesus responded to a request from the dying thief. He recognized Jesus as a king who would someday wear a real crown and wield a genuine scepter and gasped, "Remember me when Thou comest into Thy kingdom." Always open to those who wanted forgiveness, Jesus replied with majestic assurance, "Today shalt thou be with Me in paradise" (Luke 23:42-43).

Notwithstanding His utter frankness and magnetic forcefulness, Jesus Christ possessed immense warmth. He was full of mercy and tenderness, possessing the common touch for common man, inviting, "Come unto Me, all ye that labor and are heavy laden, and I will give you rest" (Matt. 11:28).

Jesus established intimacy with people quickly. His openness was reinforced by His understanding of people and of human nature. Immediately on meeting Simon He gave him a new name, showing His knowledge of Simon's area of weakness. Seeing Nathanael the first time, He recognized his honesty. In that day common people deemed religious leaders unapproachable, but Jesus rubbed shoulders with the ordinary people in the marketplace.

In Genoa, Italy, a diver, sitting on a rock and staring into the clear green water, thought, "Wouldn't it be wonderful if a statue of Christ could be placed down there? Then all who have lived by the sea and died in it would have Christ near them."

The idea raced through Genoa and far beyond. Hundreds of Italian athletes sent in bronze and copper trophies to be melted down for the statue. The Italian navy and merchant marines offered bronze scrap from Italian ships sunk in World War II.

Then for nearly a year, a 61-year-old sculptor worked to model a figure 8 feet tall to stand on a pedestal 10 feet high. The planners decided to mount the statue 56 feet below the surface of a nearby bay, where crystal clear waters would make it visible from above.

On the big day 3,000 people gathered on a flotilla of small boats to watch the giant 900-pound statue, suspended from a naval crane, lowered into the sea. Slowly the water rose, inch by inch, till at last it swirled over the outstretched hands of the statue of Christ. Later, the man who had thought up the idea, led a group of divers below with floral decorations. He surfaced, deeply moved. "I had such a lump in my throat I didn't think I could manage getting to the bottom with my carnations," he said.

To place a statue of Christ under the bay so perished sailors would have Christ near is a thoughtful gesture. But Christ is near to anyone who wants to come to Him in repentance for forgiveness. The New Testament specifically states that we don't have to climb up into heaven to bring Christ down from above, nor do we have to descend into the deep to bring Christ up. Rather, says Paul, "The word is nigh thee, even in thy mouth, and in thy heart: that is, the word of faith, which we preach; that if thou shalt confess with thy mouth the Lord Jesus, and shalt believe in thine heart that God hath raised Him from the dead, thou shalt be saved" (Rom. 10:6-11).

We don't need a statue nor a picture of Christ, for we can go to Him directly; He is so close and available. In fact, He bids us "come boldly unto the throne of grace, that we may obtain mercy, and find grace to help in time of need" (Heb. 4:16).

His Transforming Power

People surrendered their possessions and their lives under Jesus' charisma. His magnetism challenged men to follow Him completely.

Zaccheus was so moved by his encounter with Jesus that he gave away half of his goods besides restoring fourfold to those he had cheated (Luke 19:8). How poor he had been in the morning, for he was lost to God, despised by fellowmen, and agitated within. Yet at night he had peace with God, had made it right with his fellow-men, and had become a clean and useful instrument through the transforming power of his new Master.

Simon was transformed from clay to rock. Fickle and vascillating when he first met Jesus, this blundering, blustering disciple became the unshakable, reliable leader of the early church, over and over strengthening his brethren. Likewise, thunderous, fiery John became the apostle of love through his association with Jesus.

Because Mary understood the reality of His coming death, she took a very valuable box of ointment, the equivalent of a year's wages, and anointed Him in preparation for His burial. Her sacrifice is even more significant since she had not used this precious perfume to anoint her brother Lazarus at his death a few weeks before.

In His final week, Jesus' impact on others was especially evident. Where would He find a colt to ride into Jerusalem for His so-called triumphal entry? An unnamed follower let the disciples take his colt simply because, "The Lord hath need of him" (Luke 19:34).

Where would Jesus find a room in which to celebrate the Passover with the Twelve? He directed His disciples to a man who, when learning of the Master's need, immediately placed his large, furnished upper room at His disposal.

Where would Jesus be buried? Would His corpse be tossed into Potter's Field to add to His already deep humiliation? No—a secret disciple came into the open to give Jesus his own private tomb.

Jesus' magnetism has continued through the centuries. Napoleon reputedly said, "Alexander the Great, Caesar, Charlemagne, and I have founded empires depending on force, but Christ founded one on love, and to this day millions would die for Him."

Jesus said, "And I, if I be lifted up from the earth, will draw all men unto Me" (John 12:32). The old rugged cross has a peculiar fascination for people of all ages. Jewelry stores from Hong Kong to New York City display the cross as the emblem of Christianity. The cross, which symbolizes Christ's death by execution, has become a badge of honor.

Admittedly, we can never approximate the intrinsic charm and captivating loveliness of our Lord Jesus Christ. However, we are expected to exercise a gracious influence that will draw people to the Saviour. By fitting word, by kind deed, and by Christlike character we should interest others in coming to know Jesus.

A baroness, living in the highlands of Nairobi, Africa, told of a young national who was employed as her houseboy. After three months he asked the baroness to give him a letter of reference to a friendly sheik some miles away. The baroness, not wishing the houseboy to leave just when he had learned the routine of the household, offered an increase in his pay. The lad replied that he was not leaving to get higher pay. Rather he had decided he would become either a Christian or a Mohammedan. This was why he had come to work for the baroness for three months. He had wished to see how Christians acted. Now he wanted to work for three months for the sheik to observe the ways of the Mohammedans. Then he would decide.

The baroness was stunned, as she recalled her many blemishes in her dealings with the houseboy. She could only exclaim, "Why didn't you tell me at the beginning!"

We are to live so as to be Bibles, not libels. Our prayer should be the words of an old chorus, "Let the beauty of Jesus be seen in me."

8
The Loneliness
of Jesus

A tourist riding in a taxi through Times Square saw this note pinned to the back seat, "I'd rather you talk to me than tip me. I'm lonesome. Your driver." The loneliest mile in the world may be Broadway from 42nd to 59th Streets, the heart of New York City.

Two major kinds of loneliness are isolation in space, and insulation of spirit. The first type belongs to the person with no one around geographically: the fisherman alone at sea, the forest ranger in his remote tower, the prisoner in solitary confinement, or the astronaut in orbit. But the loneliness of a person isolated spatially is often softened by the knowledge that before long he will see loved ones again.

Worse is the loneliness of a person insulated in spirit. Though rubbing shoulders with crowds daily, he has no one in whom he may confide, and no one from whom he may derive understanding: some students on a major university campus, tenement dwellers in a large city, or subway travelers, swaying on straps midst jostling crowds. A best-seller bore the title, *The Lonely Crowd*. Pop tunes focus on missing relationships with such titles as "Lonely Voices."

Man is a social creature whose nature cries out for companionship. How true God's declaration, "It is not good that the man should be alone" (Gen. 2:18). Pals, clubs, marriage, the family, and

73

the church are God's answer to the longing of the human heart for friendship. More recently, ventures like singles' apartments, encounter groups, hot lines, and computerized dating services have highlighted the widespread problem of loneliness.

Loneliness afflicts all ages. A teenager who threatened to jump from the 11th floor of a Manhattan hotel lamented, "I'm alone." The feeling of not belonging is a leading factor in youth suicides. Elderly people often suffer loneliness of space and spirit too. Not only set apart in some room in a house, or nursing home, or veterans' hospital, they miss friends who have passed away, leaving few kindred spirits with whom they can find rapport.

Lord Byron wrote,

> But midst the crowd, the hum, the shock of men,
> To hear, to see, to feel, and to possess,
> And roam along the world's tired denizen,
> With none who bless us, none whom we can bless;
> This is to be alone; this is solitude.

Why are people lonely with others around? They may feel abandoned. A friendship may have shattered, a marriage fractured. Dreams may be unrealized, work unfulfilling.

Or people may feel isolated because they are either below or above the moral level of those around. Through selfishness and meanness people narrow themselves into friendlessness. Or a person may be so elevated in ideals that he cannot find kinship with his associates. Saintliness of character sets him apart. The youth who refuses to take dope may find himself forsaken by those who do. A young lady who adheres firmly to her conviction of moral purity may find herself ostracized by her sexually permissive peers. Those who dare to be a Daniel often have to stand alone.

The Lord Jesus was lonely on many occasions. His loneliness was caused by the loftiness of His person and precepts. Seldom was He alone spatially, for He was surrounded by great multitudes. But missing in the crowds was the kinship of spirit He craved. So He habitually sought the fellowship His heavenly Father could provide.

He Was Misjudged by His Family

A worker ministering to the Boston street people during the 1960s used to feed them on both Thanksgiving and Christmas days. During those two holidays suicide rates rose among the youth culture. He knew of kids who hitchhiked home at those holidays just to peer through the window of their home and see the family gathered around the Thanksgiving turkey, or the stockings hanging up at Yuletide and their mom and dad and little brothers and sisters exchanging gifts. Then, without going in or even ringing the bell, they hitchhiked back to Boston.

Jesus must have had pleasant memories of home life, surrounded by brothers and sisters and parents. The names of His four brothers are listed, plus the mention of at least two sisters (Matt. 13:55-56). Counting Jesus, this made a minimum of seven children who played together, walked to the synagogue together, ate at the same table, and enjoyed fun times in family gatherings.

Midst the joys of family life, Jesus' ideals and aspirations must have sometimes puzzled His family. But real loneliness came to Him when He left home and started His public ministry. After He began to make strong claims about Himself, perform wonders, and draw crowds about Him, His family became offended. They paid Him a visit to try to interrupt their "sick boy's" ministry. "There came then His brethren and His mother and, standing without, sent unto Him, calling Him. And the multitude sat about Him, and they said unto Him, 'Behold, Thy mother and Thy brethren without seek for Thee'" (Mark 3:31-32).

Comments Dr. Charles R. Erdman, "Here Jesus finds Himself in one of the most painful situations, one of the most delicate dilemmas of His earthly ministry. . . . The purpose of their errand has already been declared. They believe Jesus to be insane, and they are intending to stop His work. What can Jesus do? He cannot be untrue to His mission; He will not be unkind to His mother" (*The Gospel of Mark*, Westminster Press, pp. 67-68).

Jesus met the difficulty by proclaiming a timely truth, namely that the real relatives of Christ were those who did the will of God. Looking toward His disciples, He answered, "Behold My mother and My brethren! For whosoever shall do the will of God, the same is My brother, and My sister, and mother" (vv. 34-35).

Though Jesus' reply was essentially inoffensive and nonrepudiating, His words did contain a subtle rebuke. He implied that failure by His brothers and sisters to follow Him would mean they were not His spiritual kindred. Those who did His will were closer than flesh-and-blood relatives.

The rift between Jesus and His brothers widened. Later they jibed Him about going to a religious festival at Jerusalem, hinting He should present His credentials to the leaders there. "His brethren therefore said unto Him, 'Depart hence, and go into Judea. . . . If Thou do these things, show Thyself to the world.'" Then John added, "For neither did His brethren believe in Him" (7:2-5).

As a Christian teenager I was given encouragement by my parents to pursue the things of God. But some young believers aren't so fortunate. On her return from church one Sunday a young lady told her unbelieving, widowed mother that she had accepted Christ and wanted to follow Him. Her mother gave her the choice of following Christ or living at home. The daughter packed up her belongings and left.

Perhaps you have been opposed, persecuted, even disinherited because of your faith in Christ. Remember, first, that Jesus sympathizes with your loneliness. He spoke of being without honor "among His own kin, and in His own house" (Mark 6:4).

Remember too that His brothers came to believe on Him very soon, for they were gathered with the 120 in the Upper Room before Pentecost (Acts 1:13-14). His brother, James, to whom He appeared on the resurrection day, became the leader of the Jerusalem church (1 Cor. 15:7; Acts 15:13).

A young Jew accepted Jesus as his Messiah. His parents watched the transformation in his life, as he went back to college, quit dope, then became a missionary for one of the Jews for Jesus traveling teams. Though they didn't disown him, they could not accept his new occupation.

When his dad was scheduled for surgery, the young convert flew to his father's side. He reported, "I arrived at the hospital while my father was still in the operating room. When my mother saw me, she cried for joy. The operation was successful. Soon my prayers were answered. As my father was coming to, he saw me, and with tears in his eyes said, 'I'm proud of you.' Those parents came to accept my ministry and my message."

Take courage. Perhaps your family will come to trust Christ too.

He Was Rejected by His Hometown Folks

When veteran Methodist pastor and evangelist, Dr. Bob Schuller, was invited back to a school seven miles from his boyhood mountain home to preach the baccalaureate sermon, what a reception greeted him. Though the school was 22 miles from the nearest railroad stop, people came from all over the mountain country. Old men who had known him as a child sat on the front row. The building would not hold a third of the crowd. Loudspeakers carried his voice to the 2,000 people sitting on the hilltop. Dr. Schuller was thrilled.

When Jesus went back to His hometown of Nazareth to preach, His fame had already saturated the country. Old friends turned out in force to see Him. But when He finished His sermon in the synagogue where He had been brought up, His friends were offended. "Is this the carpenter's son?" they asked.

Though admitting the graciousness of His words, they "rose up, and thrust Him out of the city, and led Him unto the brow of the hill, whereon their city was built, that they might cast Him down headlong" (Luke 4:29). But passing through their midst, He escaped. Marveling at their unbelief, He could do no mighty works there (Matt. 13:58). Rejection by His acquaintances of other years must have been a bitter pill.

So, if some people cool off in their friendship because your ideals and lifestyle differ from theirs, remember that Jesus knew what it was to be lonely among friends for righteousness' sake.

He Was Misunderstood by His Followers

When misjudged by His family, and rejected by His hometown friends, to whom did Jesus turn? To the company of the Twelve. Robert E. Coleman says, "He actually spent more time with His disciples than with everybody else in the world put together. He ate with them, slept with them, and talked with them for the most part of His entire active ministry. They walked together along the lonely roads; they visited together in the crowded cities; they sailed and fished together in the Sea of Galilee; they prayed together in the deserts and in the mountains; they worshiped together in the synagogues and in the temple" (*The Master Plan of Evangelism*, Revell, p. 43). But despite all the time spent with the Twelve, Jesus was often lonely in the midst of their companionship. Was there ever a teacher more misunderstood than He?

To train men to carry His message to the world, Jesus had to choose teachable, childlike, pliable pupils. Charles Slattery wrote, "We infer that Palestine did not have a man of trained mind who was willing to be taught by Christ; else Christ would have chosen him. The prime necessity was the docility and straight simplicity of such men as He did choose to be His disciples" (*The Master of the World*, Longmans, Green, and Company, p. 220).

Jesus called His disciples friends, yet they were slow to learn. "Ye are My friends, if you do whatsoever I command you. Henceforth I call you not servants, for the servant knoweth not what his lord doeth; but I have called you friends" (John 15:14-15). They often asked Him to explain privately the meaning of something He had said publicly. They were narrow-minded, and openly rebuked parents for bringing their children to the Saviour. Repeatedly He reproved them for their carnal ambition to be prime minister in the coming kingdom. Despite their mutual love, a gaping chasm existed between Christ and His followers.

Jesus Turned to His Father

Craving human friendship but never fully finding it among the disciples, Jesus turned to His heavenly Father.

The seventh chapter of John ends with Jesus' followers going home at day's end. But verse one of chapter 8 completes the picture. Visualize Jesus and some of His disciples making their way through the Jerusalem streets at dusk after a busy day. As doors open to receive disciples for overnight, the group slowly thins out. Finally, the one remaining disciple turns into a home, bidding Jesus "shalom."

Only Jesus is left. Though in home after home families have assembled for their evening meals, the lonely Stranger walks on. No friendly door opens to Him, no kind voice beckons Him in. He passes through the city gate, and climbs the slope of Olivet to find His resting place beneath the stars in His Father's presence. "And every man went unto his own house. . . . Jesus went unto the Mount of Olives" (John 7:53; 8:1).

A painting, *The Man of Sorrows,* portrays a solitary figure, seated alone on the rocks of some mountain height, a look of inexpressible pain and longing on His upturned face. Midst the dreary waste, this homeless wanderer, rejected by family, despised by hometown folks, misunderstood by His own disciples, and scorned by His own nation's leaders, is sustained by communion with an unseen presence, His heavenly Father. The day before the cross He said to His disciples, "Behold, the hour cometh, yea, is now come, that ye shall be scattered, every man to his own, and shall leave Me alone: and yet I am not alone, because the Father is with Me" (16:32).

He Was Abandoned by His Father

But there came a time when Jesus was forsaken by His heavenly Father. On the cross His fellowship with the Father was severed. No one can know the loneliness Jesus felt then. As He was made sin for us, bearing our iniquities, the Father turned away. After three hours of dark silence, Jesus cried out, "My God, My God, why hast Thou forsaken Me?" (Matt. 27:46) He suffered the loneliness of hell that we might enjoy the fellowship of heaven.

Part of the hellishness of hell will be loneliness. The Bible pictures people in a lost eternity as "wandering stars, to whom is reserved the blackness of darkness forever" (Jude 13).

C. S. Lewis, in *The Great Divorce,* portrays hell as an ever-expanding city with an increasing number of empty streets. It happens this way: arriving people, because they're so quarrelsome, pick fights with neighbors within 24 hours. Quarrels are so unpleasant that within a week the newcomer decides to move. Likely he would find the next street empty because everyone there has quarreled. If he moves to an inhabited street, he's sure to have another argument and move on again. People keep getting farther apart. Before long they are thousands of miles from the bus stop where all newcomers from earth first arrive. By telescope newcomers can see the lights of inhabited houses of old-timers who live millions of miles away, not only from the newcomers but from each other.

Help for the Lonely

Jesus' work of redemption. Existential loneliness stems from our sense of alienation from God and resultant empty lives. Existential writers paint graphic portraits of lonely people separated from the transcendent and purposeful. The cure for this loneliness is the cross where Christ was cut off from the Father that we might be reconciled to Him, and find usefulness in His service. But we must admit our lostness and sinfulness, and turn in faith to Christ as Saviour. This decision we make alone.

Jesus' offer of companionship. Alive today, the Lord Jesus bids us seek His company. "For we have not an high priest which cannot be touched with the feeling of our infirmities; but was in all points tempted like as we are, yet without sin. Let us therefore come boldly unto the throne of grace, that we may obtain mercy, and find grace to help in time of need" (Heb. 4:15-16). Because He knows loneliness, He can sympathize with us when we're misjudged by family, rejected by friends, or misunderstood by associates.

Two sisters, Susan and Anna Warner, lived on Constitution Island opposite West Point where their father was chaplain and professor of English. Both girls were authors. Susan's book, *Wide Wide World,* sold second in copies only to *Uncle Tom's Cabin.* Besides being a prolific fiction writer, she wrote hymns including *Jesus Bids Us Shine.* She began a Bible class for West Point Cadets. She was buried in West Point military cemetery by special permission.

After Susan's death in 1885, Anna, last survivor of her family, lived alone on the island for 30 years. How easy it would have been for her to have become inert and self-absorbed. But she carried on her sister's Bible class till her death. She edited two hymnals, besides writing well-known hymns such as *Jesus Loves Me.* When someone referred to her loneliness, she replied, "I am not alone; the Lord is with me." She too was buried at West Point military cemetery with former Bible class members as pallbearers.

Jesus' provision of the church. Elizabeth Barrett Browning wrote: "How many desolate creatures on earth have learned the simple dues of fellowship and social comfort, in a hospital."

Indeed, warm relationships, developed in hospital settings between patient and nurse, or aide, or doctor, or roommate, have genuine therapeutic value.

But the church is really God's hospital, ordained for the soul-health of His followers. When a person becomes a member of the body of Christ, he enters a fellowship of concern where every believer should seek to show love for others. Psychologists tell us that stress can be handled far better by those who have a strong network of family and social ties. Without such support a person becomes a prime candidate for illness, both physical and mental.

A 9-year-old girl came home from school to find her invalid mother partly uncovered on her bed. Trying not to awaken her, she pulled the covers up to her mother's neck. Awakening, her mother smiled and whispered, "Isn't it strange? A few years ago when you were a little child, I used to tuck you in. Now you tuck me in." The daughter whispered back, "Mother, we take turns."

The pain of loneliness, high on the list of mankind's problems, can be remedied through the warmth of a caring church, whose Head knows full well the anguish of loneliness.

9
The Humor
of Jesus

The first International Conference on Humor and Laughter was held in Cardiff, Wales in 1976. Papers examined the theories of laughter, children's humor, ethnic humor, the use of humor in the classroom, and recorded laughter as used in TV comedy shows.

The second International Humor Conference, held in 1979, included a lecture by *Saturday Review* editor Norman Cousins on humor as a healing agent. He referred to his *New England Journal of Medicine* account (popularly related in his long time best-selling book, *Anatomy of an Illness*) of his remarkable recovery from a crippling disease of the connective tissue, from which doctors told him his chances of recovery were one in five hundred. Doses of laughter were a major part of his therapy. Cousins holds that the potential value of humor in medicine is virtually untapped.

The Bible recognizes the therapeutic value of humor too. "A merry heart doeth good like a medicine" (Prov. 17:22). One doctor said, "If you can't take a joke, you'll have to take medicine."

The fact that Jesus used humor may come as a surprise to some people. For several reasons we don't readily recognize His humor. In the first place, we read the words of Jesus with solemn mood, looking for values far removed from humor. Secondly, if what one generation laughs at is not considered funny by the next era, appreciation of the incongruity of situations of 1900 years ago may not be easily grasped. Finally, some never find humor in Jesus' teachings because they claim that Jesus never laughed, nor even smiled, emphasizing that He was a Man of sorrows.

Because the Gospels fail to mention the smiles and laughs of Jesus does not mean He did neither, for they give incomplete snatches of His life. Only 35 days of His entire ministry are mentioned, and then just fragments. If a full record existed, doubtless we would read of His smiles and laughs. His perpetual solemnity cannot be proved.

He was a Man of joy as well as a Man of sorrows. He wished our joy would be full. Though the shadow of the cross enveloped His ministry with gravity, the Gospels picture Him optimistic, serene, and entering into the joys of the people. He attended a wedding, resorted often to the relaxed atmosphere of the Bethany home of Mary, Martha, and Lazarus, and told a parable in which a father made merry at the return of his prodigal son. All these reflect a lightheartedness of character, despite the gloomy opinions of some people.

Though the Scripture never mentions Jesus laughing, the Gospels clearly record several statements which must have sounded funny to His hearers. Since wit and wisdom are closely allied, it's not surprising to find examples of wit in the teachings of Him who is wisdom personified. Because He knew all truth, He would be quick to note any incongruity, which is the essence of much humor. Also, if humor can be utilized as a teaching device, wouldn't the Master Teacher use it on occasion? A *Christianity Today* article says, "From the record of Scripture, Christ is never known to have laughed aloud, but a great deal that He did and said is imbued with transposed laughter as He deals in His unique saving way with the inadequacies of His friends and the enmity of his adversaries" (John W. Duddington, "The Conclusive Laughter of God," March 16, 1959, p. 13).

Jesus threw into comic relief some of the moral inconsistencies of His day that they might be seen in their proper perspective, corrected, and avoided by others. For example: Walking down the street is a man with a telephone pole protruding from his eye. Coming toward him is another man who has an almost invisible speck in one of his eyes. Then the man with the pole (or tree trunk or piece of lumber) sticking out of his eye, begins to criticize the fellow with the speck in his, "You've got a sliver in your eye! You shouldn't walk around with that speck there. You won't be able to see where you're going. Better let me pull it out!" And all the time a telephone pole projects from his own eye. Wouldn't you smile, perhaps even laugh, at the inconsistency? And wouldn't the point Jesus made be very clear, "You hypocrite, first get that piece of lumber out of your eye; then you'll see clearly to cast out the little sliver from your brother's eye"? (see Matt. 7:3-5) At times Jesus' humor seems to have been directed toward His disciples, sometimes toward His enemies, and frequently toward the indifferent. In the following cases, the samples in each category follow the usually accepted chronological order of His ministry.

Foibles of His Followers

Nicknames are often humorously revealing. Simon was anything but rock-like when Jesus first met him. His oscillating, vacillating character flared up time and time again. Yet Jesus called him Peter, which means "a rock." Andrew and other bystanders who knew Simon only too well may have snickered among themselves at that new name. Of course, our Lord knew what Simon could and would become—the strengthener of his brethren.

In choosing the 12 disciples, the Saviour gave the brothers, James and John, the surname Boanerges, which means "sons of thunder." Its aptness showed later when James and John wanted to call down fire from heaven to consume the Samaritans who wouldn't receive Jesus. *The Expositor's Greek Testament* in its comment on Mark 3:17 suggests the name "may have been an innocent pleasantry in a society of free, unrestrained fellowship, hitting off some peculiarity of the brothers."

How prone Christians are to worry. To show the absurdity of such a practice Jesus told of birds sowing in the spring, reaping in the fall, then binding the sheaves together and storing them in barns (Matt. 6:26). Can't you just see a sparrow running a threshing machine! Yet how much better than birds are God's children. Children don't worry whether or not their parents will feed and clothe them. To reinforce inconsistency of God's children failing to trust their heavenly Father, Jesus asked, "What man is there of you, whom if his son ask bread, will he give him a stone? Or if he ask a fish, will he give him a serpent?" (7:9-10)

Failure to forgive is another foible of human nature. To show the incongruity of a Christian's unforgiving spirit, the Lord spoke of a servant who owed his master 10,000 talents. After the debt was compassionately cancelled, the servant, who had 100 pence owed him by a fellow servant, mercilessly refused to grant extension of credit, and threw the debtor into prison. Our Lord's use of exaggeration is cast into clearer relief when we change the sums of money into our coinage. Using round figures, we could say that the man who was forgiven $20,000 refused to forgive a debt of $20. This gross disparity would likely evoke a smile from His hearers, at the same time teaching them that, when forgiven our enormous debt against God, we should show mercy to fellowmen whose wrongs against us are insignificant by comparison.

Picture the manager of a large business who gets his walking papers. In the week before his dismissal, while still in authority, he writes off the debts of many companies, anywhere from 20 to 50 percent of the total. He does this so that when he is unemployed these other companies will treat him kindly, even give him a job. Though disagreeing with his ethics, we would be amused at his ingenuity. Our Lord gave a story like this in which, commending the manager's zeal but not his dishonesty, He pointed out that the children of this world are wiser than Christians in their intitiative and industry (Luke 16:1-13). The emulation of zeal as illustrated in this semi-humorous story could result in reward in heaven.

Isn't there a tinge of humor in the way the risen Christ appeared to the Emmaus disciples on the afternoon of the first Easter? Two disciples are walking on the road, engaged in earnest discussion. They are recounting the events of the weekend, including the crucifixion and reports of the resurrection. Quietly Jesus joins them. Though they know Him well, they do not recognize Him. Jesus asks, "What are you talking about? And why are you sad?" Says *The Expositor's Greek Testament* in its comment on Luke 24:17, "The question of the stranger quietly put to the two wayfarers is not without a touch of kindly humor."

Recovering from surprise at the interruption of their conversation, they ask, "You must be a stranger not to know the supreme subject of the hour?" Then Jesus asks in effect, "What subject?" Isn't there another touch of humor when the very subject of their discussion stands before them without their recognition? Moreover, He walks miles with them still unrecognized, till finally He makes Himself known in the breaking of bread in their home.

Relating this episode in later months, they would not only admit their deep chagrin but also their appreciation of the humor of the situation. "And to think we were talking about Him all those miles we walked with Him, and we didn't recognize Him!"

The noted Bible expositor, G. Campbell Morgan, remarked, "There is a tender and beautiful playfulness in the way He dealt with these men. Humor is as divine as pathos, and I cannot study the life of Jesus without finding humor there" (*The Gospel According to Luke,* Revell, p. 277).

Faults of the Pharisees

The Greek word for *hypocrite* comes from two words which mean "playing the part under" a disguise. Much of Jesus' humor struck out at the Pharisees who so often tried to appear what they were not.

Ushers are passing the offering plate on Sunday morning. Suddenly a man sitting next to the aisle stands up, pulls a trumpet from under his coat, and blasts out three staccato notes. Everyone looks around in time to see him drop a $100 bill on the plate. Jesus imagined such an amusing possibility when He advised, "When thou doest thine alms, do not sound a trumpet before thee, as the hypocrites do in the synagogues and in the streets" (Matt. 6:2).

Clowns and tramps draw laughs because of their grotesquely patched clothes. To defend his disciples for feasting instead of fasting like the followers of John the Baptist, the Lord said that for His disciples to mourn while He, the Bridegroom, was present was as inconsistent as cutting out a piece of new cloth to patch a hole in an old garment. The effect would be ludicrous. Not only would the old garment look odd, but the new cloth would have a hole in it (Luke 5:36).

Our Lord gave the amusing description of wolves parading in

sheep's wool (Matt. 7:15). Wouldn't it be funny to find oranges on apple trees, or raspberries on poison ivy plants? This is the gist of Jesus' rhetorical question, "Do men gather grapes of thorns, or figs of thistles?" (v. 16)

An element of humor as well as pathos resides in our Lord's description of religious teachers of His day as blind leaders of the blind, with both guide and follower blindly falling into a hole in the ground (15:14).

Probably Jesus' hearers smiled when He pointed out to those who objected to His Sabbath healing of a woman who had been sick for 18 years, "Thou hypocrite, doth not each one of you on the Sabbath loose his ox or his ass from the stall, and lead him away to watering? And ought not this woman . . . whom Satan hath bound, lo, these 18 years, be loosed from this bond on the Sabbath Day?" (Luke 13:15-16)

Who can fail to catch the irony in Jesus' question when about to be stoned, "Many good works have I showed you from My Father; for which of those works do ye stone Me?" (John 10:32) Or when He called Herod a fox (Luke 13:32). Or when He called the Gentile rulers "benefactors" (22:25). Though one tyrant had even incorporated the word "benefactor" as a title along with his name, Jesus' listeners knew how utterly false this high-sounding title was.

Jesus described a guest at a wedding who haughtily and pompously taking the most important seat, was later forced to vacate his place of honor in deference to a more honorable guest. Others would undoubtedly laugh under their breath as in utter embarrassment he slid into a less important chair. The parable taught that pride resulted in abasement (14:8-11).

In His final week Jesus severely scorched the Pharisees for their incongruities. Imagine a housewife cleaning only the outside of the dish, and setting the table for the next meal with dishes smeared with food particles on the inside.

Or picture a secretary sitting down for her coffee break asking for a strainer to filter out any bugs that might have landed in her cup. As she starts to drink her coffee, somehow a camel steps into the cup. But it doesn't seem to bother her—she drinks the camel with the coffee. Can't you see the camel disappearing into her mouth and down her throat, hump and all? These humorous pictures, among others, fell from the lips of the Saviour (Matt. 23:24, 26).

Folly of the Indifferent

Who would build his mansion on sand at the beach? Architects never recommended erecting the Empire State Building on quicksand. Yet people build their lives on the shifting sands of man's speculations instead of on obedience to Christ's wisdom (Matt. 7:26-27).

Any preacher who explains the parable of the great supper will find his audience smiling at the absurdity of the excuses offered by those turning down the invitation.

The first man begged off because he had to examine a newly purchased piece of ground. But who examines property after the deal is closed, and in first-century darkness? The second man pled, "I have bought five yoke of oxen, and I go to prove them." But who waits till after buying animals to try them out? They might be lame or dead. The third man excused himself because he had just married. No wife becomes boss so soon after marriage. If she were new at cooking, she would have enjoyed a respite from meal preparation, and he would have been happy for a good meal. At any rate, Jesus used these excuses to show on what humorously flimsy grounds men reject God's great invitation to salvation (Luke 14:16-24).

A much visited tourist site in Toronto, Canada is a chateau which the owner never fully completed. Though the outside is finished, the man went broke before the interior was done. However, the government later finished the project, sometimes called "Pellatt's Folly" after the man who dreamed it up.

Our Lord told of a man who started to build a tower without first counting the cost. The result was just the foundation, the rest uncompleted, so that people began "to poke fun at him," according to A. T. Robertson's translation. Jesus was showing the necessity of counting the cost before rushing into discipleship (vv. 27-30).

Commentators have puzzled over the verse, "It is easier for a camel to go through the eye of a needle, than for a rich man to enter into the kingdom of God" (Matt. 19:24). Some suggest the eye of the needle is a gate to Jerusalem, before which a heavily laden camel would have to kneel and unburden itself before passing through. However, many scholars believe that to deny the literalness of the needle is to minimize the incongruity Jesus meant to convey. If so, this is another example of His humor. Can't you just see a camel with its big hump trying to squirm through the tiny eye of a needle?

Cleverly Jesus led the religious leaders to admit their wickedness in rejecting Him. He told them the parable of the householder who let his vineyard out to husbandmen, then at harvest time sent first of all servants, then his son, to collect the fruits. After relating how the husbandmen stoned the servants and killed the heir, Jesus asked, "What will the householder do to those husbandmen?"

Without realizing they were pronouncing judgment on themselves, the chief priests and elders immediately replied, "He will miserably destroy those wicked men, and will let out his vineyard unto other husbandmen, which shall render him the fruits in their seasons" (Matt. 21:41).

A few moments later it dawned on the chief priests that Jesus had been speaking of them. Bystanders must have chuckled at the way Jesus had clearly pointed out the faults to which the religious leaders themselves were blind.

We laugh when friends tell us how they ran out of gas on a trip. Or how they rose early to start on vacation only to find their gas tank empty with no nearby stations opening for hours. Jesus told of the five foolish virgins who took no oil for their lamps and missed the wedding party (25:1-10). People today are just as foolish who neglect to prepare for Christ's coming.

Jesus used humor. Since humor is integrally wrapped up with human nature, He who knew what was in man would not fail to employ it. One scholar summarizes well: "He is a man speaking to men in the language of men; and pathos, contrast, humor, and spontaneity are the natural and pleasant marks of that language. A smile is felt in His words, as in the words of all who see contradiction without loss of inner peace" (Hastings, article entitled "Humor" in Dictionary of Christ and the Gospels, Vol. 1, p. 761).

10
The Submissiveness
of Jesus

A foreigner served as physical therapist to the King of Nepal. One day as she sat in the garden with the princesses a scorpion, emerging from the flower bed, walked toward them. The princesses, with their silks rustling about them, ran in all directions. The therapist quickly took off her high-heeled shoe, chased the insect into a drain, and killed it. Trying to replace the shoe, she stood on one foot, struggling to keep her balance. Just then the king showed up. Taking in the situation, he said nothing. But he knelt on the flagstones beside her, took her foot in one hand, and put her shoe back on her foot. For a Westerner this act was a natural reaction. However, the king belonged to the second highest Hindu caste, whereas earth and feet were the defiling area of the lowly sweeper caste.

Jesus Christ, Lord of glory, was the epitome of submissiveness, yielding to His earthly father, to His heavenly Father, and to inferior fellowmen.

His Submission to Parental Authority
The first trait of Christ's character mentioned in the Gospels was submissiveness. It occurred in the temple incident when He was 12. This trait dominated His life to the finish.

On the return trip from Jerusalem after the Passover celebration the boy Jesus was suddenly missing. His frantic parents rushed back to Jerusalem to find Him sitting in the midst of the learned, dignified doctors, both hearing and asking them questions. When His parents reproved Him, He gave this amazing answer, "How is it that ye sought Me? Wist ye not that I must be about My Father's business?" (Luke 2:41-49)

Already He was aware of His messianic mission. And already He was acknowledging subservience to His Father's will. But submission to His heavenly Father meant at this point submission to his earthly father. Luke adds, "And He went down with them, and came to Nazareth, and was subject unto them" (v. 51). Despite the exhilaration of the dialogue in the temple, Jesus returned to the mundane task of obedience to His parents.

He learned a trade. Day after day He took instruction from His foster-father in the mechanics of carpentry. When He made mistakes, Joseph corrected Him.

How paradoxical—He who knew all wisdom took advice from his earthly father. He who in His preexistent state gave orders now took orders from earthly parents. Why did He submit? In His incarnate state the nurture and admonition of good parents helped Him successfully pass from boyhood to manhood.

Made under the law, our Redeemer placed Himself under obligation to keep the fifth commandment. "Honor thy father and mother" (Ex. 20:12). What an example to our rebellion-riddled society which has launched an all-out attack on the family. Of course, if parents are to be honored, they must be honorable. Paul reminded parents of their reciprocal obligation, "Provoke not your children to wrath" (Eph. 6:4). Surely God selected godly parents for the upbringing of His eternal Son. And the Son responded by submitting to them.

If a child learns respect for the first authority he faces in life, his parents, he is more likely to obey other authorities he meets later. Martin Luther said, "What is a city but a collection of houses? Where father and mother rule badly, and let children have their own way, there neither city, town, village, district, kingdom, nor empire can be well and peacefully governed."

The child who honors his parents will more readily respect his teachers, obey the laws of the land, defer to his employer, and obey the Gospel. We're not surprised to see Jesus, as He moved out from under parental roof, urging obedience to human government. "Render therefore unto Caesar the things which are Caesar's" (Matt. 22:21). He paid the temple tax (17:24-27). He attended synagogue worship regularly (Luke 4:16). He did not neglect the regular feast days (John 2:13; 7:14). After healing lepers, He bade them follow the Law, "Go show yourselves unto the priests" (Luke 17:14).

Only when duty to His heavenly Father ran counter to earthly regulation did He violate human authority. His disciples, Peter and John, ordered by the Sanhedrin not to speak the name of Jesus, rather declared their intent to obey God, not men. But where no conflict arises, the Christian is obligated to follow Jesus' example of willing obedience to constituted authority.

His Submission to His Heavenly Father

Our Lord's submission to His heavenly Father meant the temporary abdication of His celestial home. How much more pleasant to enjoy the privileges of heaven than to suffer the deprivations of earth. But "Christ pleased not Himself" (Rom. 15:3). He left the many mansions of His Father's house, often finding no place to rest His head.

Submission to His heavenly Father meant poverty. Though He owned the cattle on a thousand hills, yet for our sakes He became poor. At His infant dedication, His parents brought a dove in place of the costly lamb, an alternative offering permitted the poor. During His public ministry He depended partly on the financial support of women (Luke 8:2-3). When the disciples were hungry, they plucked corn from the fields, a practice allowed hungry travelers as part of a Jewish program for the poor. At the end of His life, Jesus had no possessions except the clothes on His back which were divided before His eyes. He was buried in a borrowed tomb.

Submission to His heavenly Father also meant inconvenience. Crowds robbed Him of His privacy. One day He was so tired He fell asleep in a boat midst a violent storm and had to be awakened because of the danger (Mark 4:36-41). Another day He sat weary by a well, letting the disciples make the trip into town to buy food (John 4:6-8).

What an example to us today to be willing to answer a call for service, though it means getting dressed up, leaving a favorite book, chair, or television program, and taking time and energy to go somewhere out of our way to make a visit, or attend a meeting. A middle-aged couple with no children were asked to pick up a little boy from a broken home who wanted to go to Sunday School each week. Because it meant rising earlier, driving several blocks out of their way, perhaps getting the car dirty from wet feet on rainy mornings, and hampering their frequent Sunday pleasure trips, they said no. People are not willing to be tied down, whereas Jesus was willing to be "nailed" down. Repeatedly He surrendered whatever plans He may have had to solve the problems of others.

Submission to His heavenly Father meant limitation. Though the incarnate Christ did not relinquish His deity, He did forego the independent exercise of His attributes. For example, though omnipresent, He became subject to the limits of space. Though omniscient, He learned like other children.

Similarly, Christians are often called on to temporarily surrender certain rights. "We then that are strong ought to bear the infirmities of the weak, and not to please ourselves. Let every one of us please his neighbor for his good to edification" (Rom. 15:1-2). We are asked to follow in the train of Christ who on leaving heaven for His earthly ministry exclaimed, "Lo, I come . . . to do Thy will, O God" (Heb. 10:7).

In the early 1960s Rev. Leymon W. Ketcham, better known as "Deak" from his days of college sports, moved from the vice-presidency of The Kings College to the Directorship of Development at Gordon College. In 1966 he learned that he had a terminal illness. He reacted with an attitude typical of his entire Christian life. "If that's what the Lord has for me, it's all right with me." His final weeks were a radiant testimony to medical personnel and friends.

Statement after statement especially in the Book of John proves Christ's total submission. When John wrote, "He must needs go through Samaria," it was not because of usual geographical routing, for the Jews usually avoided Samaria. Jesus went that way to fulfill His Father's plan (John 4:4).

Repeatedly Jesus clearly stated that He never acted outside of the jurisdiction of His Father's will. He said, "My meat is to do the will of Him who sent Me, and to finish His work. . . . For I came down from heaven, not to do Mine own will, but the will of Him that sent Me. . . . My doctrine is not Mine, but His that sent Me. . . . I speak to the world those things which I have heard of Him" (John 4:34; 6:38; 7:16; 8:26).

Nothing Jesus said or did stemmed from His own private whim. Even His baptism was an act of submission "to fulfill all righteousness" (Matt. 3:15). As His life was ending He said, "I have finished the work which Thou gavest Me to do" (John 17:4).

Absolute surrender to the divine will was the controlling factor in Jesus' life. He continually gave consent to the Father's orders, all summed up in His Gethsemane acquiescence, "Not My will, but Thine, be done" (Luke 22:42). Jesus' commitment to the Father's program climaxed at Calvary. When the mob at the cross derided Him, "He saved others, Himself He cannot save" (Matt. 27:42), they spoke the truth. Since the Father's will required death as the price for man's forgiveness, Jesus had not come to save Himself but to give His life as a ransom for us (Mark 10:45).

The lesson of Jesus' obedience was not lost on the Twelve. When he said, "As My Father hath sent Me, even so send I you" (John 20:21), they knew they would have to obey like their Master. As 20th-century servants of Christ we must not dilly-dally around with His commands. The Hebrew understanding of knowledge is no mere accumulation of biblical facts, but the degree to which we integrate truth into our lives.

When Rev. Wally Holder, a New Hampshire pastor, had serious voice trouble, he consulted a throat specialist. Given some exercises to do, Holder resisted the doctor's orders. "I thought that if keeping silent for the few previous weeks hadn't helped, surely exercising my vocal cords wouldn't help either. Then I began to follow instructions. When I submitted to his directions, then my voice improved." He added, "Isn't it often this way in our relationship with the Lord? So often we resist His will, even when it's the best thing for us."

Submission to His Fellowmen (really His inferiors)

When a young couple, newly appointed missionaries, arrived at the mission's branch office, they were met by a perspiring man in shirt-sleeves who carried their bags up to their room. Later they were quite surprised on meeting the branch director to find the same man who had so kindly carried their suitcases.

The New Testament enjoins a submissive spirit for followers of Christ. Paul wrote for us to be "submitting yourselves one to another in the fear of God" (Eph. 5:21). Peter expressed the same truth, "All of you be subject one to another, and be clothed with humility" (1 Peter 5:5).

The inspiration for total submission of course is the example of the Lord Jesus, who though very God became a servant. This attitude is to control us (Phil. 2:5-7).

The Lord of glory stooped to serve mankind in various ways. He taught, preached, and healed. He broke the bread and distributed it to His disciples in both feeding miracles. He replenished the refreshments at the wedding in Cana. He broke the bread and handled the cup at the Last Supper. On the seashore after the resurrection He prepared the fire, and seemed to be the cook. Peter described Him as one "who went about doing good" (Acts 10:38). Though He was really Master over all, yet He was also servant, answering the call for help and ministering to the needy.

The concept of Christ's submissiveness so strongly permeates early Christian thinking that the titles given church leaders signify service. Apostle means "sent one." A minister is one who serves. The noun *deacon* comes from a verb which means "to serve." A bishop is an overseeing servant. Leaders are not bosses, but servants. Both Paul and Peter called themselves servants of Jesus Christ (Titus 1:1; 2 Peter 1:1).

During a flood that took over 200 lives in Rapid City, South Dakota, in 1972, survivors were taken to a high school gymnasium for medical care and rest. The head nurse realized that a major source of infection might be the bare feet of those who, asleep when the wall of water cascaded through the city, had their feet dirtied by the rampaging mud. So, students in the high school's Department of Practical Nursing volunteered to go from cot to cot with basin and towel, carefully washing the feet and medicating the wounds of the injured.

Our opportunities to follow Jesus, who washed the feet of His disciples, will not be the same literally, but will be abundant. We are to relieve those suffering illness and pain, help the mentally distressed, give hospitality to strangers, visit the aged, comfort the sorrowing, befriend outcasts, and feed the hungry. Even the insignificant cup of cold water given in Jesus' name will not go unrewarded.

It goes against human nature to take a subordinate position. We enjoy sitting in the driver's seat. Though we claim our drive for a position of power is the desire to have a free hand to do good, honest introspection often reveals the real motive—ego gratification. But the Lord taught His followers to relinquish the higher seat for a lower place.

In one of his letters, Peter urges a submissive attitude by using Jesus' subjection to unjust treatment as a model (1 Peter 2:21-25). Then the apostle spells out several relationships calling for this subordinate behavior.

Because of Christ's example citizens are told, "Submit yourselves to every ordinance of man for the Lord's sake; whether it be to the king, as supreme; or unto governors" (vv. 13-14).

To servants, Peter writes, "Be subject to your masters with all fear; not only to the good and gentle, but also to the froward" (v. 18).

Wives are advised, "Likewise ye wives, be in subjection to your own husbands" (3:1).

Husbands also have a responsibility, "Likewise, ye husbands, dwell with them according to knowledge, giving honor unto the wife, as unto the weaker vessel, and as being heirs together of the grace of life" (v. 7).

All believers are included in Peter's command for mutual submission, "Finally, be ye all of one mind, having compassion one of another, love as brethren, be pitiful, be courteous" (3:8).

Power struggles occur in all relationships of life. Labor strikes are often expressions of resentment at management's careless use of power. Workers want more say in the decision-making process. On the other hand, unions often restrict the authority of supervisors, making their jobs unattractive and difficult.

Many church fights stem from groups vying for power, hiding behind such rationalizations as "standing for the truth." But the Lord Jesus made no power plays. He refused to yield to the devil's lure of gaining sway by turning stone into bread, floating down from the temple to land uninjured, or by becoming ruler over all earthly realms (Matt. 4:1-11). Rather, He chose to operate from a position of weakness—the shameful cross. He was born lowly, died in weakness, and won through serving.

Often in home life, wives resent doing menial tasks while their husbands sit watching TV. And husbands who have it hard enough taking orders at work worry over the feminine challenge to their authority at home.

After a couple undressed for bed on their wedding night, the bride spotted some clothes on the floor of their motel room. "What's that?" she asked.

"My underwear," the groom replied. "My mother always picks it up and washes it."

"Well, I'm not," retorted the bride.

The next morning the underwear was still on the floor. The second morning there were two pairs of men's underwear there. At end of their week's honeymoon seven pairs sprawled on the floor. The couple left the underclothing there.

Returning to their new apartment, the groom took a $200 gift certificate from their wedding presents and bought $200 worth of underwear at Sears. When he had thrown all these new sets of underwear on the bedroom floor, they decided the conflict was serious enough to see a counselor (at a fee of $50).

Hearing them out, the counselor asked the husband, "If your wife bought a hamper, would you be willing to throw your dirty underwear in the hamper?"

"Why, sure," replied the groom.

Turning to the wife, the counselor asked, "If your husband threw his underwear in the hamper, would you be willing to wash it?"

"Yes, I would."

They went out and bought a hamper. The problem was solved.

(Very likely that couple would have to learn the lesson of submission several times on their road to marital happiness.)

God created us to have relationships. Growth comes through loving others, which at times means submission, and esteeming others better than ourselves. Too often we react, "Imagine me lowering myself to do that! Don't people know who I am?" Cutting right through such an attitude is the humility of the Son of God who voluntarily placed Himself under the Father's domination. Instead of grasping at His rightful honor of equality with God as a prize to be held at all cost, He made Himself a servant. As a result of His total submission, the Father has exalted His Son above every name.

During a depression a kind baker sent for 20 children, each from a poor family in town. Pointing to a pile of loaves, he told the children to take just one each. They pushed and shoved to find the biggest loaf. When all had run off without a word of thanks, one little girl picked up the small loaf that was left, then thanked the baker.

The next day the same thing happened, except when the little girl's mother cut into the loaf, out fell a pile of silver coins. She sent her daughter back to the baker with the coins. Said the baker, "It was no mistake. I put the coins in the smallest loaf to reward you."

The Lord has promised to elevate the submissive. May this mind be in us, which was also in Christ Jesus.

11
The Graciousness
of Jesus

A century ago a poor orphan in a small German town advertised a piano recital. Her posters falsely identified her as a student of the famous Hungarian composer and pianist, Franz Liszt. To her horror she learned that Liszt was going to visit her town at the time of her recital. Knowing he would certainly see the posters, she dreaded the serious consequences. With a step of real courage she requested an interview with the celebrity on his arrival just the day before the concert. She sobbed out her confession, anticipating well-deserved reproof.

Said Liszt, "You certainly have done a very wrong thing, but we all make mistakes. Then the only thing to do is to be sorrv. I think you are sorry. So let me hear you play."

Playing in front of the master frightened her so she stumbled quite a bit at first, but gaining more confidence, she played better. After correcting her in a few places, Liszt remarked, "I have now instructed you a little. You are a pupil of Liszt. You may go on with your concert tomorrow night. The last number will be played, not by the pupil, but by the teacher."

Such kindness is but a faint reflection of the graciousness of the Lord Jesus Christ in His undeserved favor toward the disadvantaged, the poor, the powerless, and the sinful.

In the prologue to his Gospel, John speaks of Jesus as "full of grace" as well as of truth (1:14). Luke in speaking of His growth as a child in stature, spirit, and wisdom adds, "and the grace of God was upon Him" (Luke 2:40). After His return to His hometown synagogue, all "wondered at the gracious words which proceeded out of His mouth" (4:22). These gracious words may have referred to His verbal charm, but perhaps also to the wide range of unfortunates who were to be the recipients of His love. He had just mentioned His anointing to preach the Gospel to the poor, to heal the brokenhearted, to preach deliverance to prisoners and recovery of sight to the blind, and to set at liberty the bruised (v. 18).

From the very outset He demonstrated His non-statistical regard for people. Everyone was a somebody. His kindness extended to all classes alike—from the coarse, blundering fisherman, Peter to the cultivated Sanhedrinist, Nicodemus. Jesus identified with the lowly, the least, the last, and the lost.

His first miracle relieved the predicament of a young couple who ran out of wedding refreshments. How embarrassing if the word got around. Guests may have whispered, "They should've planned it better. Maybe they can't really afford to get married!" Had Elijah or John the Baptist faced that situation, they might have given the couple a lecture on the wickedness of wine or warned that enough was enough. But the Lord graciously performed the miracle behind the scenes so that even the host was surprised.

Jesus' gracious manners controlled His speech. Most of us periodically engage in loud conversation, yelling at our children, or at drivers who cut in front of us. Though on rare occasion the Lord shouted some important truth (John 12:44), His voice was usually calm and subdued. Isaiah had predicted His soft-spokenness, "He shall not strive, nor cry; neither shall any man hear His voice in the streets" (Matt. 12:19). He was patient with His disciples, permissive with those undecided, and even polite to His enemies.

So gentle was the Lord that it was declared, "A bruised reed shall He not break, and smoking flax shall He not quench, till He send forth judgment unto victory" (Matt. 12:20).

A frail reed, though already bruised and vitality sapped, He would not finish breaking. Those bowed down with penitent unworthiness and bruised by the blows of life the tender Christ would not injure more nor destroy, but would strengthen instead.

When a lamp wick began to burn dimly and smoke thickly, the tendency was to quickly extinguish it. But when the flame flickered in the hearts of those on the verge of spiritual extinction, the mild Christ would not blow even softly, lest He snuff out the dying flame. He never snapped anyone's spirit.

Womanhood

Long before Women's Lib, Jesus honored womanhood. His keen sensitivity to the plight of widows shines through the sacred record. He spoke of the widow who cast her all into the treasury, and of the unfairly treated widow whose importunity finally moved an unjust judge to action. He even raised from the dead the only son of a widow of Nain.

Women were not only His followers but His financial supporters as well. "Certain women, which had been healed of evil spirits and infirmities, Mary called Magdalene, out of whom went seven devils, and Joanna the wife of Chuza, Herod's steward, and Susanna, and many others . . . ministered unto Him of their substance" (Luke 8:2-3).

Women were last to leave the cross, and first at the empty grave. How gracious for the risen Christ to make His first appearance to a woman, and to one who had previously been demon-possessed.

One very strict sect of the Pharisees, termed "Bruised and Bleeding" Pharisees, thinking women the cause of lust, not only refrained from talking to women, but also closed their eyes so as not to see them at all. Naturally this resulted in walking into walls, thus their name. How shocked they were one day when a woman with a city-wide reputation as a sinner came unbidden into Simon the Pharisee's house where Jesus was a dinner guest. The woman began to wash the Lord's feet with her tears, and to wipe them with her hair. The emotional warmth must have been quite embarrassing. Wouldn't His "testimony" be fractured by allowing a loose woman to touch Him? But He defended her against Simon's cynicism by rebuking the Pharisee for his pride and lack of thoughtfulness in not washing Jesus' feet (Luke 7:36-50).

Not long before the cross, Mary, sister of Martha and Lazarus, in gratitude broke a box of ointment and poured it over Jesus' head. As the ointment flowed down to His feet, the disciples began to realize its cost, roughly the equivalent of a year's wages. They whispered jibes among themselves, led by Judas, "What a waste! It ought to have been sold, and the proceeds given to the poor!" Mary became confused and deflated. Was she wasteful? Had she erred?

Knowing her act sprang from love as advance burial preparation, the Lord kindly explained how much this offering meant to Him. His suffering and death were not far off. Though the poor would always be present, the occasion to help Him face His ordeal was only temporary. Her act would be immortalized in the sacred record. How Mary must have rejoiced at His appreciation (John 12:3-8).

Clumsy clergymen might have given the magnanimous lady a lengthy sermon on the wise use of money, the dangers of extravagance and the pitfalls of waste, all broken down into three main points with subdivisions. She would have been humiliated, while the preacher might have prided himself on his courageous speaking out. But in reality, blindness would have missed the generosity of her act.

The Physically Disadvantaged

The graciousness of Christ was markedly evident in His dealing with the handicapped and ill. How readily He expended the necessary energy in restoring men whole. Never more at home was He than in a crowd of persons suffering every type of disease and deformity. Moving among them compassionately, He touched some, spoke to others with a word of power, revealing gentleness as He healed them.

When a lady with a 12-year blood disease touched the hem of His garment and was instantly healed, the Lord didn't point her out roughly, "Hey, woman, you just touched Me and got rid of your blood disease." Rather, with great sensitivity He said, "Who touched Me? I perceive that virtue has gone out of Me." He let her come into the open on her own to worship and testify (Luke 8:43-48).

When Jesus healed a deaf man with a speech impediment, He took the victim aside from the crowd, providing privacy for his first attempt to speak plainly, and for his first experiences at hearing the wonders of sounds and voices (Mark 7:32-37).

It showed grace for Jesus to touch the unattractive, diseased, and unsanitary, for He could have healed them with a wave of His hand. It especially took graciousness to touch lepers who had to cry out "Unclean!" when anyone approached. Since lepers lost their sense of touch in the affected areas, the touch of Jesus would make human contact meaningful again.

A student on an Oregon campus during the rebellious '60s always looked the same—mussed hair, blue jeans, T-shirts, and never any shoes, even in rain or snow. He became a Christian about the time a middle-class church near the college decided to minister more to students. One morning the student walked into the church in his usual garb, and without shoes. Some members looked a little squirmy as he moved down the aisle looking for a seat. The church was filled, so reaching the front pew and seeing no empty seat, he just squatted on the carpet—usual procedure at college fellowships, but somewhat disconcerting for a fashionable church.

Tension rose. Suddenly a man walked down the aisle toward the boy. He was a member of the church board. Would he lecture the lad? The boy's friends sitting elsewhere thought the man was about to remove him. But when the official reached the student, with difficulty he managed to squat down beside him on the carpet. As both worshiped on the floor that morning, few eyes were dry.

His Own Disciples

A maid picked up the ringing phone. Before she could say a word, the voice at the other end began to yell and curse. She recognized the person as the man of the house. When she managed to get a word in, he realized his mistake. "So sorry, I thought you were my wife."

Sadly, people are often more gracious with strangers than with their loved ones. But not our Lord. He was most considerate of the Twelve. How ironic that the night before He died, He was comforting the disciples. They should have been comforting Him in the face of His ordeal. But it was He who said, "Let not your heart be troubled" (John 14:1).

With full knowledge that they would forsake, flee, and deny Him, "having loved His own which were in the world, He loved them unto the end" (13:1). Even at the moment of His arrest he thought of their welfare, saying to the officers, "If therefore ye seek Me, let these go their way" (18:8). In grace He caught Peter's eye at his third denial, melting Peter to bitter tears. On the resurrection morn, knowing that Peter had died a thousand deaths in those intervening hours, Christ had the angels give this message to the women, "Go . . . tell His disciples and Peter" (Mark 16:7). How this must have revived Peter's spirit!

How courteous Jesus was to Judas, hiding his identity as traitor almost to the end, instead of making a grand public announcement days in advance. At the arrest Jesus even called him "comrade," permitting the betrayer to kiss Him. Generously He restored Malchus' ear which clumsy Peter had cut off with his sword.

In the midst of His agony on the cross He made arrangements for His mother's future, entrusting her to the care of the Apostle John (John 19:26-27).

He invited doubting Thomas to put his finger in the nailprints, condescending to submit to Thomas' prestated test (20:24-28).

After the disciples' fruitless night of fishing, Jesus gave them directions which resulted in a catch of 153 fish. In addition, He invited them to breakfast He had made for them on the shore (21:5-13).

Despite their denials and desertions, He forgave them through His marvelous, matchless grace. Dr. Vernon Grounds of Denver Conservative Baptist Seminary tells of a pastor who left the ministry because of immorality, backslid, and then deliberately moved into a Jewish community. Trying to get away from his Christian past, he changed his name to a Jewish one. Then he married a Jewish girl who didn't know his background. A Jewish mission started in the area. His wife had to walk by the mission building every day. One day she went in. Interested, she kept returning. You can guess what happened. She was converted. When she told her husband, he broke down and cried like a baby. God wouldn't let him go. Where sin abounded, grace did much more abound. Restored, he became useful in Christian service again.

The Undecided

Though Christians should possess a passion for souls, we observe that Jesus Christ did not seem to buttonhole everyone in sight with the question, "Are you saved?" On occasion He took the initiative, but more often people sought Him out. Indiscriminate witnessing seems to find little practice in our Lord's ministry. He was led of the Spirit. Perhaps for us a winsome disposition under the power of the Spirit would draw people seeking spiritual direction.

When we try to persuade others to our way of thinking we often become argumentative, harsh, and authoritarian. But the Lord never strove—He was gentle to all men, meekly instructing those that opposed the truth. Nor did He press or beg for immediate decision. His invitations to conversion were always permissive. Explaining the new birth to Nicodemus, He gave time for the good seed to become fruit. Though grieved when the rich young ruler turned away from Him, the Lord didn't pressure him into remaining.

Would-be disciples found Jesus' demands of discipleship high. Instead of coercing people to come after Him, Jesus restrained people from following Him unless they had counted the cost. He didn't apply pressure for decisions. The Spirit of God, symbolized by a dove, never destroys the personality of an individual, but causes it to blossom and unfold instead of crushing it into subjection. God's aim is to get people genuinely regenerated and dedicated, rather than count scalps by picking unripe fruit.

Sinners

Christ's graciousness is no more vividly displayed than in His forgiveness of penitent sinners. Grace has been succinctly defined as undeserved favor. Sinners deserve hell, but through the grace of Christ may receive heaven.

More than once our Lord set Himself between public sinners and the accusing finger of society. One day the scribes and Pharisees dragged a woman to the feet of Jesus, accusing her of adultery. She must have stung with shame, especially since they had seized her in the very act. Declaring that Moses commanded such sinners to be stoned, they asked Jesus for His verdict. Jesus simply stooped and wrote with His finger on the ground. When they continued to bombard Him with questions, He rose and challenged those without sin to cast the first stone. Stooping again, He resumed writing on the ground. No one knows what He wrote, perhaps nothing but doodling. But whether aimless scribbling or meaningful message, His action certainly revealed His kindness. It diverted attention from the humiliated woman. The eyes of the Pharisees that had focused on her face now gazed at the sand. The convicted Pharisees began to slip away one by one. How gracious and merciful was the conduct of Christ.

Then came the word of pardon, "Woman, where are those thine accusers? . . . Neither do I condemn thee: go and sin no more" (John 8:2-11). Just as Christ's healing touch checked the course of physical disease, so His forgiving word stopped the bondage of sin, enabling her to turn away from her evil life and resist temptation.

Another woman with whom the Master dealt kindly was the Samaritan. Some Christian workers, on discovering her marital status, would have immediately launched into a discourse against immorality. But Jesus, starting with a request for a drink of water, gently swung into her past, pointing out that she had had five husbands. His approach was so tactful that she didn't seem to mind that He told her everything that she had ever done. She became an effective witness among her own people. "Many of the Samaritans . . . believed on Him for the saying of the woman" (4:5-39).

A pastor noticed a stranger lighting up her cigarette during a special ladies' evangelistic luncheon in his church fellowship hall where smoking was not permitted. His immediate impulse was to send word for her to stop. But the guest-speaker whispered to the pastor, "She's the only one doing it. She'll stop in a few minutes anyway. Why embarrass a stranger?" The pastor restrained himself. Deeply moved by the sermon, the lady began attending church, became a believer, and later the Sunday School superintendent. The pastor often wondered if she might have been turned off had he not followed the gracious suggestion of the guest-speaker that day.

Jesus' magnetism drew Zaccheus, chief tax collector of Jericho, to climb a tree to see what Jesus looked like. Jesus knew this and called out, "Zaccheus, make haste, and come down; for today I must abide at thy house" (Luke 19:5). As Jesus walked with Zaccheus toward his home, the stunned crowd murmured that Jesus was going to be a guest of a notorious sinner. As the murmuring buzzed more loudly, the situation became embarrassing. Some of us would have been tempted to lecture Zaccheus on his need for restitution and charity, but Jesus patiently gave him time to express himself. His gracious treatment paid off, for Zaccheus announced his intention to make amends.

Zaccheus' interest in Jesus may have come from reports from other tax collectors. Perhaps ex-publican Matthew had circulated word to those in his profession that Jesus came to a dinner where most guests were tax collectors. And how in answer to the Pharisees' criticism, "Why eateth your Master with publicans and sinners?" He had given this revolutionary reply, "I will have mercy, and not sacrifice: for I am not come to call the righteous, but sinners to repentance" (Matt. 9:10-13).

Though Jesus openly declared God's laws, He conveyed them so warmly and lovingly that He became known as the "friend of publicans and sinners" (Luke 7:34). Today many of us would avoid any place where sinners congregate, but in His day Jesus drew near sinners. When the Pharisees complained that Jesus received and ate with sinners, He related three parables, all of which had to do with the joy of finding lost things. The shepherd rejoiced when the lost sheep was rescued. The housewife delighted when her lost coin was recovered. The father ran to embrace his prodigal son on his return home. The elder brother who sulked was out of tune with his father who ordered the best robe, shoes, and fatted calf for a party celebrating the prodigal's homecoming. The Pharisees' failure to exult over the repentance of the lost publicans showed an attitude far removed from the gracious spirit of Christ.

I worked my way through Moody Bible Institute by writing for its radio station, WMBI. A weekly program for which I was responsible, *Trophies of Grace,* began with this announcement, "Stories of men and women whose lives were deep in sin, but who were transformed by the power of Christ. Lives where sin abounded, but where grace did much more abound." As I prepared those dramatizations of God's saving goodness in the lives of people who had been vile and immoral, I never ceased to marvel at the grace which could wipe out every deed, no matter how dark the sin or how deep the stain.

Years ago a man was driving through Europe in a Rolls Royce when it developed mechanical difficulties. Rolls Royce headquarters in England sent two mechanics by plane to the continent to repair the engine. When the owner received no bill, he wrote the factory about the cost of the repair job. Came the answer, "We have no record of any mechanic flying to Europe to repair your car. In fact, we have no record of any mechanical difficulty ever occurring in a Rolls Royce."

Man, in dire need of spiritual repair, may find through the grace of Christ that not only is every sin forgiven, but every vestige of iniquity is removed from the divine record.

12
The Vitality
of Jesus

Gazing at a painting of Jesus in an art gallery, a visitor commented, "Almost looks like an invalid!"

Too many representations of Christ, figments of medieval imagination, portray Him as some sort of weakling on the verge of illness, smiling wanly under an ethereal halo.

Healthy Man

He must have had a strong, robust constitution. His rigorous schedule demands could only have been met by a person in vigorous condition. Interviews, long periods of teaching, the drain of energy from healing the crowds whom He sometimes touched one by one, journeys, mountain climbing, nights in prayer, sojourning in the rugged wilderness of Judea where severe climatic conditions took the life of controversial Bishop Pike a few years ago, all suggest a sturdy physique. We visualize Him toughened by the toil of carpentry and bronzed by the blazing sun.

He must have had a strong voice to be heard by the thousands, out-of-doors, without the aid of loud speaking equipment. Far from nervous, He was able to sleep during a violent storm.

He endured the cross, one of the most painful agonies known to man. Some claim His rapid death indicated a weak body. However, no man took His life from Him, but He mandated the exact time of His own passing.

Rugged youths were attracted to Him by His strength, courage, and ideals. It took a man's man to cleanse the temple and drive out the money changers single-handedly. Willingly His young admirers, likely in their 20s, left home and occupation to tramp miles of sun baked paths to follow Him.

Moral Ascendency as Well as Physical Vigor

John's prologue says, "In Him was life" (1:4). Though His body was often the avenue through which His healing power traveled, His real strength came from His inner personality. He declared Himself to be the Light, Bread, Water, and Resurrection. He said, "Without Me, ye can do nothing" (John 15:5). "Because I live, ye too shall live" (14:9).

Casual friends may be fooled about our character. But our constant companions will rip off fronts, remove cover-ups, and reveal blemishes. Yet after three years of close and continual scrutiny, Jesus' disciples could not discover the slightest trace of wrongdoing. For example, Peter affirmed that He "did not sin, neither was guile found in His mouth" (1 Peter 2:22).

Moreover, Jesus gives the picture of a person in control. He was afraid of neither man nor devil. He didn't hesitate to unmask evil and pronounce woes on hypocrites. Facing His trial with its false charges, illegal procedures, scheming skullduggery, He came off as a silent King in charge of events. Even midst the torture of crucifixion He issued a pardon for His tormentors, answered a repentant thief, gave instructions for the care of His mother, announced the completion of His mission, and with dignity dismissed His spirit. He triumphed over the grave. Announcing He possessed all power, He commissioned His disciples to carry the Gospel to the ends of the earth, promising, "I am with you always, even unto the end of the world" (Matt. 28:20). Then, defying the law of gravity, He ascended into heaven.

Power over Nature, Disease, Demons, and Death

Sudden storms on the Sea of Galilee did not daunt Jesus. He could easily walk on tempestuous waves. Or with the command, "Peace, be still," He could calm the troubled waves and send the howling wind back to its mountainous caverns.

He could turn water into wine, or with a handful of loaves and fish feed thousands of hungry people. At His word the lame leaped, the blind saw, the deaf heard, the dumb spoke, the leper was cleansed, the withered limb was made complete, and the fever departed.

Demons recognized Him, crying out, "What have we to do with Thee, Jesus, Thou Son of God? Art Thou come hither to torment us before the time?" (Matt. 8:29)

Even the forces of decomposition were reversed by His power. Jairus' daughter dead less than an hour, the widow of Nain's son in his funeral procession on the way to the cemetery, and Lazarus in the grave four days, were all called back to life by the command of His voice.

Authority in Teaching

Jesus was a master teacher. He knew His subject, His audience, and how to communicate. But the outstanding factor was His commanding manner. Several times in the Sermon on the Mount He corrected misinterpretations of the Old Testament, asserting "But I say unto you." No wonder at the end "people were astonished at His doctrine: for He taught them as one having authority, not as the scribes" (Matt. 7:28-29).

Boldness

He resisted the wilderness temptations of the devil, bidding him, "Get thee hence, Satan" (Matt. 4:10). He endured the taunts of His brothers. He stood up against the Pharisees in their legalistic observance of the Sabbath, not hesitating to pluck grain or heal on that day. He refused all the trick questions of the scribes, turning the tables on them with His incisive talk, so that finally "no man was able to answer Him a word, neither durst any man from that day forth ask Him any more questions" (Matt. 22:46).

When warned that Herod was out to kill Him, He undauntedly called Herod a "fox," asserting nothing could deter Him from completing His task (Luke 13:31-33).

Despite numerous attempts on Christ's life, John reported, "He speaketh boldly" (7:26). His vitality was exhibited at His arrest. When He asked the soldiers, "Whom seek ye?" they answered "Jesus of Nazareth." At His reply, "I am He," they fell backward to the ground (18:4-6).

Not surprisingly, the boldness of the disciples indicated to the persecuting Sanhedrinists that these "ignorant" men had been associated with Jesus (Acts 4:13).

Divisiveness

Jesus' personality was so strong that people lined up either on one side for Him, or on the other against Him. On three occasions John states "there was a division" because of Him (7:43; 9:16; 10:19).

Christ is still the great divider today. Painfully but clearly He predicted, "Suppose ye that I am come to give peace on earth? I tell you, Nay; but rather division" (Luke 12:51). Then He added that a person's foes would be those of his own household.

His critics accused Him before Pilate of stirring up the people (23:5). Though delightful, He was also exasperating, often producing a crisis by compelling people to decide one way or another.

Determination

His vitality revealed itself in His commitment to do the job for which He came. He refused the offer of all this world's kingdoms to bypass His mission.

The Greeks who sought an audience may have been trying to lure the Master to go with them as a teacher. But Jesus realizing a corn of wheat to be productive, must fall into the ground and die, prayed to His Father for help, adding, "but for this cause came I unto this hour" (John 12:24-27).

In Gethsemane the possibility of rescue by thousands of angels crossed His mind. But with determination He prayed, "Not as I will, but as Thou wilt" (Matt. 26:39, 53).

Jesus could have stayed in Nazareth all His life, or avoided the hostile territory of Herod or Pilate, or refrained from messianic claims and contentious statements. But never once did He swerve from the cross before Him. "Instead, He steadfastly set His face to go to Jerusalem" (Luke 9:51).

Jesus Christ was a vigorous person, robust in health, impeccable in character, a giant among contemporaries, authoritative in His teaching, fearless in the face of demon or man, compassionate with the sick and poor, dominating nature and death, unstoppable in His resolution to finish His mission, and freely dispensing His "Be of good cheer" that brought forgiveness and joy to so many. Where did He get His vim and vigor?

Sources of His Vitality

His vitality flowed from His knowledge of His person, His origin, purpose, and destiny. Also, strength sprang from His saturation with the Old Testament Scripture.

He knew who He was. Many people flounder in life because they don't know who they are. Christ had no identity problem. At the age of 12 He already had some inkling of His person and mission, as shown in His answer to His parents for staying behind to talk to the temple teachers, "Wist ye not that I must be about My Father's business?" (Luke 2:49) He knew that He is the Christ, the Son of the Living God (Matt. 16:16).

He taught that His words would outlast heaven and earth (Matt. 24:35), that believing on Him gave eternal life (John 6:47), that He would answer prayer made in His name (14:14), that He could forgive sin (Luke 5:20), that some day He would raise the dead (John 5:28-29), and that He would judge the world (Matt. 7:21-24; John 5:22).

Three times His Father's voice announced from Heaven, "Thou art My beloved Son": at His baptism (Luke 3:22), at His transfiguration (Luke 9:35), and at the visit by the Greeks (John 12:28).

He was conscious of a special identity with His heavenly Father. No one could know the Father unless the Son revealed the Father to him (Luke 10:22). Nor could anyone come to the Father but through the Son (John 14:6). He said, "I and My Father are one" (10:30). Because the people clearly understood Him to claim equality with God, they took up stones to kill Him (5:18; 10:30-33).

Charles Eliot, former president of Harvard University, was born with a birthmark that disfigured much of his face. His first awareness of his handicap came when, as a small boy at play with neighborhood children, their cruel taunts sent him home to look into the mirror at his blemished face. His grief was uncontrollable. The next morning his sympathetic mother took him aside and spoke gently, "We've consulted the best doctors, and they say nothing can be done. But it is possible for you to grow a soul so gracious that people will forget to look at your face. Do it, son, with God's help." Eliot followed his mother's advice, becoming honored and cherished by men of learning the world over.

Believers in Christ should have no identity problems. We are sinners whose blemishes have been washed in the blood of Christ through His grace. Possessors of new life, we have been placed in the family of God, now joint-heirs with Jesus Christ. Knowing our position as children of God should provide great impetus for vibrancy in the Christian life.

He knew where He came from and why He was here. His origin was heaven. He once said, "Before Abraham was, I am" (John 8:58). He also prayed that God would glorify Him with the glory He had with the Father "before the world was" (17:5). He asserted, "I proceeded forth and came from God" (8:42).

Jesus knew His purpose. Though in coming He revealed the Father (John 1:18), identified with our deprivations in order to sympathize with us (Heb. 4:14-16), and showed us ideal man, His supreme purpose for coming to earth was to reconcile lost men to a holy God (Matt. 20:28). He knew He would be lifted up and would shed His blood for the remission of sins (Mark 14:24).

Likewise, the child of God who, realizing he is here for a reason, dedicates his time, talent, gifts, money, mind, and energy to do God's will, will find great strength from living with purpose.

He knew where He was going. Knowing the grave could not contain Him, Jesus predicted His resurrection. He also knew He would return to His Father, in the place of many mansions (John 14:1-3). He knew that at the end of the age He would return to earth in great glory to rule where He had been rejected on His first visit.

"Hereafter shall ye see the Son of man sitting on the right hand of power, and coming in the clouds of heaven" (Matt. 26:64).

He was confident that He would eat with His disciples in the coming kingdom, also that they would sit as judges on 12 thrones (Luke 22:14-18; 28-30).

Assurance of ultimate victory enabled Him to stride across the pages of history with strength and dignity. Despite adverse circumstances which might have fractured the spirit of others, our Lord stood firm and strong, with quiet vitality, deterred by nothing. At the end He could say, "I have finished the work which Thou gavest Me to do" (John 17:4). Because of the joy set before Him, He endured the cross, then sat down on the right hand of the throne of God (Heb. 12:2).

Of all people on earth only the child of God has guarantee of a glorious destiny. Because Christ lives, the believer should be able to face tomorrow. This hope should supply a flow of vitality for abundant living.

He drank deeply of the Word of God. Jesus believed implicitly in the Bible of His day, the Old Testament. He declared, "The Scripture cannot be broken" (John 10:35). Not the smallest minutia (jot nor tittle) would go unfulfilled (Matt. 5:18). He placed His stamp of approval on the historicity of several events questioned by skeptics through the centuries, including Noah and the flood (Matt. 24:37-39), Sodom's destruction (Matt. 11:23), and Jonah and the fish (Matt. 12:40).

More than believing the Old Testament record, Jesus studied it. Approximately 9 percent of Jesus' words in the four Gospels are quotes from the Old Testament, coming from over 20 books. He corrected the devil when the arch-demon misused Psalm 91 (Matt. 4:5-7).

More than believing and studying the Old Testament, Jesus applied it personally. He won victory over the devil by answering his temptations with "It is written," three times quoting from Deuteronomy (Matt. 4:4, 7, 10). He used the Word to ward off the potential entrapments by the Sadducees and Pharisees (Matt. 22:23-40).

Jesus used His Bible for encouragement and strength. The exaltation of Joseph after mistreatment by his brothers, the choice of Moses to suffer with God's people rather than enjoy the pleasure of sin for a season, the example of the suffering prophets, and the courage of Daniel all provided inspiration for His ministry.

Since in a unique way the Old Testament spoke of Him, Jesus found guidance therein. Perhaps His study threw light on the path He was to trod. On the cross, as He reviewed His life, He knew "that all things were now accomplished" (John 19:28).

It is surmised that Jesus never possessed a full Old Testament of His own. He learned from His father at work, from His teachers at rabbinical school, and from His mother whose Magnificat reveals wide knowledge of the Old Testament. Many sentences from the law and prophets sank into His mind to germinate later.

Do we prize our Bibles enough today? Not many centuries ago copies of the Bible were rare, costly, and separated into several scrolls too bulky to be combined in one volume. Some believers would never handle a copy. Then for a while it was against the law to have a Bible. Today we pick up the entire Bible in one compact volume, even pocket editions, and purchase it in several translations at cheap prices, in our own language.

Guidance for daily living can be found in Holy Writ. As we read, we should ask if there's an example to follow, like Joseph's resisting the amorous advances of Potiphar's wife. Or is there a sin to shun, like envy? Or a promise to claim, or some truth to learn about God, Christ, or the Holy Spirit.

The executor of an estate was processing the papers of a deceased man who had the reputation for godliness. Was it real? Opening his Bible, the executor found unmistakable evidence of diligent study. Every page carried marks of faithful usage, well-worn paper, choice texts underlined. The source of his virtue was evident. Sad to say, many believers are more familiar with the pages of *TV Guide* than with the words of Scripture.

The Transmission of His Vitality

Jesus never wrote a book, but libraries are full of books written about Him. He never composed a song, but His life has been the theme of compositions by Bach, Beethoven, Handel, Haydn,

Mozart, and Mendelssohn. The finest paintings highlight episodes of His life. Stately structures have been erected in His name.

He never founded a school, but numerous colleges have been established because of Him. He did not practice medicine, yet He has been the inspiration for countless hospitals.

Every dated letter, document, bill, and newspaper, written or published in the Western Hemisphere, acknowledge the influence of Jesus Christ, for the year is understood to be A.D., which stands for "anno Domini"—year of the Lord.

Napoleon said, "I have inspired multitudes with such a devotion that they would have died for me, but to do this it was necessary that I should be visibly present. But across a chasm of 1800 years Jesus Christ makes a demand which is, above all others, difficult to satisfy. He asks for the human heart. He demands it unconditionally, and forthwith it is granted. In defiance of time and space the soul of man with all its power becomes an annexation to the empire of Christ. All who sincerely believe in Him experience that remarkable supernatural love toward Him. This phenomenon is unaccountable; it is altogether beyond the scope of man's creative powers. Time, the great destroyer, is powerless to extinguish the sacred flame" (Quoted by Liddon, *The Divinity of Our Lord,* p. 150 and quoted by Robert E. Speer in *The Man Christ Jesus,* pp. 241-242).

Jesus Christ is as much alive today as when He walked the paths of Galilee. His vitality still flows on. In His final discourse He told His disciples that it was necessary for Him to go away, for thereby He would send the Holy Spirit to live in them. Thus, through the regenerating and indwelling power of the Spirit untold millions through the ages have lived with a new zest, facing danger, dungeon, fire, and sword with Holy Ghost boldness, and exhibiting Christlike character in home, community, and nation.

A new convert, an up-and-at-'em, successful young Jewish businessman on a trip to Puerto Rico, arrived at a hotel in San Juan only to find he had no room due to a mix-up in reservations. It was nearly midnight. The desk clerk, after fussing around for a few minutes, said they had a room for him at another hotel a block-and-a-half away. He lugged his baggage to the other hotel. When he arrived, they said they had no room.

The young Christian said to himself, "Here I am, not getting angry. Normally I should be going berserk, yelling at the hotel clerk and making a scene."

Just then the hotel clerk learned that a room on the third floor had been cancelled. Since the elevator wasn't working, the young believer carried his bags two flights up. The room was occupied. Downstairs again. The clerk apologized, "I made a mistake."

Frustrated, soaking wet with sweat, totally exhausted, the new convert muttered, "I can't believe it. I'm not losing my temper. I'm not blowing my top. I'm just not the same fellow." He still exhibited the same calm spirit till a room became available an hour later.

G. K. Chesterton claimed that the world is growing older and older, while the church is getting younger and younger. He meant that the vibrancy of our faith is fresh each morning with new energy and hope. Christ's vitality—His warmth, graciousness, tenderness, compassion, mercy, kindness, and love—can be ours today.

The Gift of Joy

How do you find joy? How are joy and happiness related? How are they different? In this book, Dr. Flynn dispels the myths that joy equals happiness and that grumpiness equals holiness.

God's Will: You Can Know It

How do you go about finding God's will? How can you be a decisive person—yet at the same time know you are following God's leading? From biblical principles—and the experiences of people of the past and present—you can learn how to let God direct you.

Joseph: God's Man in Egypt

Joseph was a perfect candidate for anger, despair, revenge, and self-pity. Yet Joseph's life offers hope—you too can live with courage and faith when everything around you goes wrong.

19 Gifts of the Spirit

Examine the gifts and special abilities given to Christians by the Holy Spirit. Which ones do you have? Are you using them? Dr. Flynn guides you in an in-depth study of what the Bible says about spiritual gifts.

The Twelve

What were the disciples like before they met Jesus? How did He change them? In this book, you'll discover the unvarnished truth about the ordinary men Jesus chose.